50 ways to improve your Italian

Valeria Malandra

For UK order enquiries: please contact Bookpoint Ltd,
130 Milton Park, Abingdon, Oxon OX14 4SB.
Telephone: +44 (0) 1235 827720. *Fax:* +44 (0) 1235 400454.
Lines are open 09.00–17.00, Monday to Saturday, with a 24-hour
message answering service. Details about our titles and how to
order are available at www.teachyourself.com

For USA order enquiries: please contact McGraw-Hill Customer
Services, PO Box 545, Blacklick, OH 43004-0545, USA.
Telephone: 1-800-722-4726. *Fax:* 1-614-755-5645.

For Canada order enquiries: please contact McGraw-Hill
Ryerson Ltd, 300 Water St, Whitby, Ontario L1N 9B6, Canada.
Telephone: 905 430 5000. *Fax:* 905 430 5020.

Long renowned as the authoritative source for self-guided
learning – with more than 50 million copies sold worldwide –
the *Teach Yourself* series includes over 500 titles in the fields of
languages, crafts, hobbies, business, computing and education.

British Library Cataloguing in Publication Data: a catalogue record
for this title is available from the British Library.

Library of Congress Catalog Card Number: on file.

First published in UK 2010 by Hodder Education, part of
Hachette UK, 338 Euston Road, London NW1 3BH.

First published in US 2010 by The McGraw-Hill Companies, Inc.

This edition published 2010.

The *Teach Yourself* name is a registered trade mark of
Hachette UK.

Copyright © Valeria Malandra 2010

Typeset by MPS Limited, A Macmillan Company.

Printed in Great Britain for Hodder Education, an Hachette UK
Company, 338 Euston Road, London NW1 3BH, by XXX.

The publisher has used its best endeavours to ensure that the URLs
for external websites referred to in this book are correct and active
at the time of going to press. However, the publisher and the
author have no responsibility for the websites and can make no
guarantee that a site will remain live or that the content will remain
relevant, decent or appropriate.

Hachette UK's policy is to use papers that are natural, renewable
and recyclable products and made from wood grown in sustainable
forests. The logging and manufacturing processes are expected to
conform to the environmental regulations of the country of origin.

Impression number   10 9 8 7 6 5 4 3 2 1

Year   2014 2013 2012 2011 2010

Dedication and acknowledgements

I would like to dedicate this book to my parents and my sister, whose enthusiasm and hard work have been the inspiration for all I have done so far.

I would like to thank all my students, past and present, for their passion for Italian and clever questioning.

Last but not least, I would like to express my appreciation and gratitude to editors Ginny Catmur, Sarah Butler and Jenny Gwynne, for their invaluable help in putting this project together.

Photo credits

Front cover: Oxford Illustrators Ltd.

Back cover: © Jakub Semeniuk/iStockphoto.com, © Royalty-Free/Corbis, © agencyby/iStockphoto.com, © Andy Cook/iStockphoto.com, © Christopher Ewing/iStockphoto.com, © zebicho – Fotolia.com, © Geoffrey Holman/iStockphoto.com, © Photodisc/Getty Images, © James C. Pruitt/iStockphoto.com, © Mohamed Saber – Fotolia.com

Contents

Meet the author

What is learning a language all about? I believe that it is about enjoying the process, rather than rushing to reach an end result. Of course, the prime motivation for learning a language is communication, which is a valuable goal in itself; but at its best, learning a language is also a never-ending voyage of discovery, driven by curiosity about the world and the pleasure of discovering something new.

I teach Italian to students at the University of Surrey, in Guildford, UK. When I studied foreign languages myself, in Italy – learning English, French and Spanish – I became well aware of the impact that good and bad teaching can have, and also of how much students themselves can drive and inform their learning process. I realized that an inspiring teacher can change somebody's life, but that students too play an essential part by being receptive and open to new ideas and taking ownership of the learning process.

Both teacher and student should learn from each other, forming a virtual circle. That concept lies at the core of this book: my students' constant questions, their mistakes and ways of improving, all feed into the quest to fine-tune my teaching methods in order to convey the Italian language more effectively.

Valeria Malandra

Only got a minute?

I'm sure you know that **bambino** means *child*. Let's imagine you want to ask somebody *Have you got any children?* Does the question **Ha bambini?** sound OK to you? If it does, I need to make you aware of something: Italian actually has two words for *child*: **bambino** and **figlio**. Now, what is the difference?

A **bambino** is a young child who is not yet a teenager (or, if the tone is ironic, an adult who hasn't grown up). By contrast, **figlio** means *child* in the wider sense of *offspring*, and could be of any age. It can also indicate a male child – as opposed to **figlia**, a female child.

So if you ask a woman in her 80s **Ha bambini?**, clearly the question is inappropriate as she is unlikely to have children who are **bambini**! On the other hand, you can safely ask her **Ha figli?** And of course, you can ask someone in their 30s **Ha bambini?** and that will be perfectly acceptable.

The aim of this book is to make you aware of many such subtleties of the Italian language. The example opposite is a simple error in the choice of vocabulary, but the book also covers many common errors in pronunciation and grammar.

By analyzing examples of real mistakes made by learners of Italian, you will soon see what's wrong, learn the better versions and be able to speak and write Italian more like a native speaker.

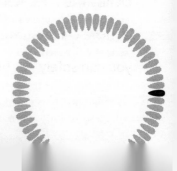

5 Only got five minutes?

It isn't always possible to find an exact equivalence or correspondence among the words we find in the vocabulary of two foreign languages. If that were so, languages would just parallel each other and wouldn't be half as fascinating.

A language tends to reflect different aspects of the environment and culture of the social group in which it is used. Each language is formed and works in such a way as to allow the most efficient communication between speakers of a shared social group, reflecting their needs, customs, culture, as well as the characteristics of their natural environment. That is why learning a new language broadens our mind and is a voyage of discovery that adds a new dimension to our life.

Let's take a verb as an example. In English there is only one verb, *to play*, to express the act of playing a game and playing a musical instrument, whereas in Italian there are two: **suonare** (*to play a musical instrument*) and **giocare** (*to play a sport/a game/a trick*):

Suono la chitarra.	*I play the guitar.*
Gioco a tennis.	*I play tennis.*

English speakers need to know that distinction to choose the correct word and make sense when communicating in Italian.

Problems can arise when learners go for words similar to English words. A classic example is translating *sensible* as **sensibile**, which actually means *sensitive*! *Sensible* should be translated instead as **sensato** or **assennato**.

Along the same lines, students will instinctively translate *village* as **villaggio**. This is correct if the village is outside Italy, but if the village is in Italy, no native speaker would say that; they would say **paese** or **paesino** instead: **un bel paesino** (*a pretty little village*). However, you might hear **villaggio** in fixed expressions such as **villaggio turistico** (*holiday camp*).

Another example: public conveniences in Italy will often have the word **Toilette** on the door or on a sign indicating the way. So English-speaking students assume that, when asking for directions to the toilets in Italy, they should say:

Scusi, dov'è la toilette? ✗

This will instantly single you out as a foreigner, as native speakers would say instead one of these:

Scusi, dov'è il bagno? ✓	*Excuse me, where is the toilet?*
Scusi, dove sono i bagni? ✓	*Excuse me, where are the toilets?*
Dove sono i servizi igienici?	*Where are the toilets?*

The foreign-import word **toilette** may be used in written language or in formal speech, but would seem odd in normal conversation.

To take one final, and more subtle, example: **poco** is often used wrongly, mainly owing to the fact that in Italian it tends to have a negative connotation. It doesn't just mean *a little*, but goes further to imply *not enough* or *not too much* of something:

Ha pochi amici.	*He doesn't have many friends.*
Ha fatto poco per me.	*He has done little for me.*
Poca pasta per me!	*Not too much pasta for me, please!*

Going beyond the meaning of words to get to the nuances behind them is part of the challenge and fascination of learning a language. This book will help you go further into many aspects of Italian vocabulary, as well as its structure and pronunciation, to increase your enjoyment and success in learning the language.

10 Only got ten minutes?

Languages are tools that we use to communicate within a wide social group. They are constantly changing: every language is a mixed language and remains alive by absorbing what it needs from other languages and cultures as time passes, making communication richer and more effective. Being alert to these changes can be both valuable and fascinating for learners.

This introduction first offers examples of the many changes that have taken place – and are indeed still taking place – in the language spoken in Italy today. Second, it focuses on a topic central to many visitors' experience of Italy – food – with examples of the most common errors made by foreigners when buying, eating or discussing food in Italian.

It's worth pointing out that languages change in the following cases:

▶ when the change will help improve communication (which is what happened in Italy when people switched gradually from Latin to Italian);
▶ when a previously united society divides (a typical example is what happened with the fall of the Roman Empire);
▶ when one society comes into contact with others, speaking different languages, that have more cultural prestige, authority or power (through invasion, occupation or more benign financial or commercial types of influence).

Interestingly, many English words were already in use in Italian by the end of the nineteenth century, as in the case of **sport** and **bar**. So much so that in the 1940s the fascist regime tried to impose an 'Italianization' of all foreign terms. For instance, the word **sport** had to be replaced by the word **diporto**.

The majority of words of English origin penetrated into the Italian language in the 1950s, after the Second World War, when American culture and lifestyle acquired increasing strength and prestige, and American fashion, cars and domestic appliances became popular in Italy.

English words that have become part of Italian are usually kept identical in the way they are written and pronounced. However, some have acquired a more general meaning or alternatively a more specific one: for instance, the word *Miss* in English is the title used for an unmarried woman or girl, whereas in Italian a **miss** is a woman or girl who wins a beauty contest! **Film** in Italian only means *movie*, whereas in English it also refers to the thin strip of cellulose used to make negatives and slides.

Many of the words Italian has borrowed from English remain the same in Italian. The most common are:

bar   computer   sport   hobby   bestseller   baby-sitter   film

However, please remember that *football* does need to be translated!

il calcio   *football*

Weekend can be used as it is, **il weekend,** or be translated as **il fine settimana**. Both versions are common. Note the use of the masculine article **il**, owing to the fact that **fine settimana** is a direct translation of the masculine word **weekend**. But the word **fine**, taken in isolation, is feminine, so if you'd like to say something like *Towards the end of the week I'll give you a ring*, you need to revert to the original gender of the word: **Verso la fine della settimana ti telefono.**

Another word derived from English is **toast**, which can stay as it is (particularly in bar menus), or be translated as **panino tostato** or **pane tostato**.

Website can be left in English or translated as **sito web** (or simply **sito**) or **portale**.

An email translates as **una mail**. The feminine gender of this word originates from the fact that *mail* translates as **posta**, which is indeed a feminine word.

For email addresses, the symbol @ is increasingly called **at**, just as in English (but the 'a' of **at** sounds like the 'e' in *pet*!). Other people seem to prefer the Italian version **chiocciola**, so it is really a matter of preference. By the way, the word **chiocciola** means *snail*! And the slash symbol (/) used in website addresses is often called exactly that, although again the pronunciation of the 'a' is slightly distorted and sounds like the 'e' in *sledge*. The Italian version is **barra**.

The letter of the alphabet **J** deserves a special mention. Nowadays a growing number of people spell out this letter as the English *jay*. But the Italian spelling **i lunga** is of course still in use.

FOOD MISCONCEPTIONS: SAY IT RIGHT OR YOU MIGHT END UP EATING THE WRONG THING!

You'll find below a whole host of words that foreign speakers tend to get wrong when talking about food.

▶ The translation of *cream* is **panna**. If you ask for **crema**, you are asking for something that is similar to custard, made with flour, egg yolk, sugar and milk, a bit like *crème anglaise*.

▶ When buying home-made ice-cream (**un gelato artigianale**) do not ask for scoops! There is no easy translation for 'scoop' in Italian; you could perhaps say: **vorrei tre palline** (*I'd like three little balls*) but it doesn't sound particularly nice and, more importantly, no native speaker would say such a thing! So, when buying **un cono** (*a cone*) or **una coppetta** (*a tub*), the amount of ice-cream you get depends on its price, i.e. how big the tub or cone is. What you should say is:
Vorrei un cono piccolo/medio/grande/da X euro.
Vorrei una coppetta piccola/media/grande/da X euro.

▶ Don't forget, the English dish *spaghetti bolognese* in Italy is called **spaghetti al ragù**.

▶ **Peperoni** in Italian are *peppers* (vegetables), not *salami* or *pepperoni*! And note that the Italian spelling only has one **p**.

▶ The English word *courgettes* is commonly translated as **zucchine**, like the American English term; in Italy it's by and large used as a feminine word, with an **e** at the end for the plural. **Zucchini** with an **i** does exist but is not as frequently used. If you do an internet search (restricting the results to pages coming from Italy and not the whole world!), you'll see that the word **zucchine** gets many more hits than **zucchini**.

▶ When ordering in a restaurant, remember the difference between a starter and a first course. In Italian the starter is called **antipasto** and the first course is called **primo** (a main course consisting of pasta or soup). Hence, **primo** is not a starter.

▶ **Insalata** translates as *salad*, but can also be used to indicate *lettuce*. Therefore, you can go to the market and simply ask for **insalata**. If you are looking for other particular types of salad, then you will need to be more specific.

▶ The translation for grapes is **uva**, which is singular, not plural as in English:
Vorrei dell'uva.   *I'd like some grapes.*

Try not to confuse **uva** (*grapes*) with **uova** (*eggs*) – take care when pronouncing the vowels.
Vorrei delle uova.   *I'd like some eggs.*

By the way, the Italian word for *egg(s)* is irregular – the singular is masculine but the plural is feminine:
l'uovo   (masculine singular)   *the egg*
le uova (feminine plural)   *the eggs*

▶ Speaking of gender, remember that **carne** (*meat*) is feminine: **la carne**. This is quite important because if you say 'il carne' you run the risk of being misunderstood for saying *the dog*, particularly as English speakers tend to pronounce the 'r' very softly. If you use the wrong word for *the*, you might end up telling people you like eating dogs!

Mi piace mangiare il ca(r)ne. ✗	*I like eating the dog.*
Mi piace mangiare la carne. ✓	*I like eating meat.*

▶ English speakers have a tendency to talk about *food* using the word **cibo**. This is fine in written or formal style, but in normal spoken conversation it would be better to use a phrase that contains **mangiare** in some form:

Non ho avuto cibo tutto il giorno. ✗	
Non ho mangiato niente tutto il giorno. ✓	*I haven't had any food all day.*
Devo comprare cibo. ✗	
Devo comprare da mangiare. ✓	*I need to buy food.*

▶ If you are ordering sparkling mineral water, don't say *with gas*. No native speaker uses that expression and it doesn't sound very elegant either!

acqua minerale con gas ✗	
acqua minerale gassata ✓	
acqua minerale frizzante ✓	
Vorrei una bottiglia di acqua minerale gassata/frizzante. ✓	*I'd like a bottle of sparkling mineral water.*

▶ Finally, did you know that dining **al fresco** doesn't mean having a table *outside*? **Al fresco** in Italian means *in a cool place* (temperature-wise). Funnily enough, it is also an idiomatic slang expression that had its heyday a few years ago and means *in prison*!

Having been introduced to some of the most common mistakes that learners of Italian make, you are now ready to start the journey full on! Enjoy yourself – **Buon divertimento!**

How to use this book

My career as a teacher of Italian started in 1995 and, over the years, I have become acutely aware that certain mistakes tend to occur much more frequently than others. This book aims to address this problem and put an end to those very common mistakes that all students make from time to time. If not properly confronted, these mistakes risk becoming entrenched and remaining unresolved even at advanced level. They might not always hinder communication, but they would be spotted immediately by a native speaker and would single you out as a foreigner who hasn't quite mastered the language.

I suggest you revisit this book several times, until you develop sufficient familiarity with its contents to enable you to stop yourself in your tracks and recognize what you are about to get wrong. By reading through the mistakes outlined in the book, you will start questioning and revising your models, which will lead you to speak and write better Italian. This book doesn't repeat the full tables of rules, verb endings and grammar patterns that you already have in your coursebook or textbook, so do turn to those reminders in other reference books whenever you need to. Instead, this book goes straight for the most likely problems and picks out the most interesting points of the language.

This book is divided into three main sections, focusing on different areas: pronunciation and spelling, structure, and vocabulary. The grammatical terms used in the book are explained in a glossary at the back; there is also an index of all the key points to help you quickly find what you want.

Physicist Niels Bohr once defined an expert as a person who has made all the mistakes that can be made in a very narrow field; so don't worry about making mistakes. In order to succeed, you must repeatedly fail. But becoming aware of each mistake is an essential step towards avoiding it in future.

In his book, *The decisive moment,* Jonah Lehrer writes: 'If we can't incorporate the lessons of the past into our future decisions, then we are destined to endlessly repeat our mistakes.' This concept encapsulates very effectively the rationale behind this book.

Now a word of caution. Too often, conventional grammar books are devoid of any doubt or ambiguity on the part of the author; they attempt to systematically list all the rules and regulations that form the basis of any given language. The reality is that grammar is full of exceptions and irregularities. Some rules are so vague and fluid that it would be more appropriate to talk about 'tendencies' or 'trends'. Where a rule can indeed be identified, there might be regional variations to take into account, or exceptions intervening in a specific context or at a specific time. So it is important not to ask too much from a grammar book, but rather to keep an open and searching mind. Remember that learning a language is a long-term undertaking: you can only master it one step at a time.

This book will analyze real mistakes that no Italian native speaker, using standard Italian, would normally make. Those incorrect sentences are indicated in this book by a cross: ✗
You need to learn the correct versions, indicated with a tick: ✓

This book won't always be able to tell you why a particular example is wrong, as it may simply be one of the many idiosyncrasies of the language, with no conclusive explanation: in these cases, it simply 'is', and the best you can do is be aware of it and aim to get it right.

Useful links
http://italianoecc.blogspot.com/
Author's lively blog offering bite-sized items of interest on Italian language and culture.
www.teachyourself.com
This website has a recording demonstrating pronunciation points made in this book, a set of multiple-choice questions to help you practise, and a set of articles about language and culture.

Sounding right

1a Good stress and bad stress

Stress gives more prominence to a syllable, by way of loudness, pitch or length.

In Italian there is no simple way to predict where stress falls in a word; there are many rules and exceptions and of course native speakers don't learn them at school but simply acquire them by being constantly exposed to the language. The single most important rule to learn is that most words are stressed on the penultimate syllable – the last but one. (A syllable is a minimum combination of sounds.)

The word **domani** (*tomorrow*) has three syllables **do-ma-ni,** and the stress falls on the penultimate syllable: **ma**. The stress is indicated in this chapter by underlining those letters.

Listen to the examples in the online audio recording available at: www.teachyourself.com

Some Italian words are written with an accent, a graphic sign showing where the stress falls. If a word ends with an accented character, you need to make sure that your voice marks the stress on that syllable by reinforcing the sound. Try saying out loud the wrong (✗) and right (✓) versions of these words, to feel the contrast:

città ✗	città ✓
università ✗	università ✓
età ✗	età ✓
metà ✗	metà ✓
nazionalità ✗	nazionalità ✓
lunedì ✗	lunedì ✓
martedì ✗	martedì ✓
mercoledì ✗	mercoledì ✓
giovedì ✗	giovedì ✓
venerdì ✗	venerdì ✓

But the vast majority of Italian words don't use accents to signal where the stress falls. This is why it can be tricky to get the stress right, especially when it follows an irregular pattern. Keep in mind that the basic pattern is for the stress to be on the last-but-one syllable.

These Italian words are regularly mispronounced by students at all levels:

sabato ✗	sabato ✓	*Saturday*
suocera ✗	suocera ✓	*mother-in-law*
fegato ✗	fegato ✓	*liver*
la famiglia Medici ✗	la famiglia Medici ✓	*the Medici family*
Mi piace leggere. ✗	Mi piace leggere. ✓	*I like reading.*
gonne leggere ✗	gonne leggere ✓	*light skirts*
	vestiti estivi ✓	*summer clothes*
	Vestiti, è tardi! ✓	*Get dressed, it's late!*

1b Good stress and bad stress

We saw in the first two pages of Chapter 1 that it's easy to mispronounce the stress in Italian words. While this may simply make it harder for people to understand you, with some words moving the stress changes the meaning. We saw this clearly in the two meanings of **vestiti**: *clothes* and *get dressed*.

Two other common pairs of words are also easily confused if you get the stress wrong:

leggere   *to read* (verb)

As opposed to:

leggere   *light* (adjective)

and:

papa   *the pope*
papà   *dad, daddy*

Notice that the stress may not be marked with a visible graphic sign – you just have to learn the correct pronunciation.

WORDS ENDING IN -IA

Now notice where the stress falls in many words ending in **-ia**:

Ungheria   *Hungary*
macelleria   *butcher's*
gelateria   *ice-cream shop*
scrivania   *desk*

This is not always the case though. Some words ending in **-ia** follow a different stress pattern:

malaria   *malaria*
veterinaria *veterinary*

STRESS IN VERBS

Stress is also troublesome when it comes to verbs that look very similar, as in the case of **tagliare** (*to cut*) and **togliere** (*to remove/take off*). It's also tricky when it comes to verb conjugation, although here there are useful patterns to help you. Read these columns out loud and notice where the stress falls in the present tense of the verb **abitare** (*to live*) and **visitare** (*to visit*), as opposed to a shorter verb like **vedere** (*to see*):

present tense		
(io)	**abito**	**visito**	**vedo**
(tu)	**abiti**	**visiti**	**vedi**
(lui)	**abita**	**visita**	**vede**
(noi)	**abitiamo**	**visitiamo**	**vediamo**
(voi)	**abitate**	**visitate**	**vedete**
(loro)	**abitano**	**visitano**	**vedono**

Another typical situation where the syllable stresses seem to run wild is the imperfect tense. Notice that the stress follows the usual pattern (penultimate syllable) for all the persons <u>except</u> the very last one:

imperfect tense		
(io)	**abitavo**	**visitavo**	**vedevo**
(tu)	**abitavi**	**visitavi**	**vedevi**
(lui)	**abitava**	**visitava**	**vedeva**
(noi)	**abitavamo**	**visitavamo**	**vedevamo**
(voi)	**abitavate**	**visitavate**	**vedevate**
(loro)	**abitavano**	**visitavano**	**vedevano**

Insight

In the present and the imperfect tenses, the sound in the stressed syllable in the **loro** form is the same as in all the singular forms: **abito/abiti/abita, abitano, abitavo/abitavi/abitava, abitavano**.

Also note that the **noi** and **voi** forms of the present tense are always stressed on the first part of their endings: **-amo** and **-ate**, no matter what comes before that ending.

2 Soft and hard sounds

An extremely frequent mistake occurs when soft and hard sounds are mixed up, i.e. when soft sounds are pronounced in a hard, guttural way, and vice versa.

In English, an example of a hard sound is the **c** in *cat*, as opposed to the soft sound of **ch** in *chair*. As the letters **ch** in English make a soft sound, learners of Italian fall into the trap of applying the same sound to Italian words. So the beginning of a word such as **chiesa** (*church*) is wrongly pronounced with a **ch** sound as in *cheese*:
chee-eh-zah ✗

The right pronunciation is:
kee-eh-zah ✓

Similarly, a word like **schema** (*scheme*) is often mispronounced:
sheh-mah ✗

You should be saying instead:
skeh-mah ✓

In Italian the following clusters of letters make hard guttural sounds, like the English 'k/g/sk':

ch	ca	co	cu
gh	ga	go	gu
sch	sca	sco	scu

Here is a list of words that have those hard sounds:

chilo	pistacchio	chiave	chiacchierare
tartarughe	Ungheria	larghe	leggo
schema	dischi	schiena	rischio
bruschetta	pesche	schermo	scuola
scacchi	finisco	esco	scuola

The following clusters of letters make a soft sound, like the English 'ch/j/sh':

ci   ce   gi   ge   sci   sce

Here is a list of words with those soft sounds:

**ciao invece giovedì leggere scienza
finisce esce pesce scegliere**

The word **ghiaccio** (*ice*) contains a hard **g** and a soft **ch**.
gee-ah-cho ✓

Here are wrong (✗) and right (✓) ways of pronouncing the common word **pesce** (*fish*), which invariably 90 per cent of students get wrong at some point in their learning process:
peh-skeh ✗   peh-sheh ✓

Similarly, many students have a moment of hesitation when reading out **faccio** (*I do/I make*), and end up choosing the wrong pronunciation:
fah-kkio ✗   fah-cho ✓

Another common mistake is to pronounce the letter **c** as an **s**. Consider these ways of saying **necessario** and **decido**:
neh-seh-sa-reeo ✗   neh-cheh-sah-reeo ✓
deh-see-doh ✗   de-chee-doh ✓

The letter **c**, in isolation, is pronounced 'chee', and by the same token, a **CD** is to be pronounced 'chee dee'.

One last point relates to the tendency among English speakers to make the **t** too soft and breathy, adding a hint of a 'ch' sound.
For instance, **quattro** becomes:
koo-ah-ch-tro ✗

Keep it clean and sharp: remember that a **t** is only ever pronounced as a **tee**!
koo-ah-ttro ✓

3a Say it like you write it

Putting stress aside, Italian pronunciation is actually very simple and consistent: the way you write it and the way you say it coincide. But often the learner's mother tongue or knowledge of other foreign languages will play havoc.

DOUBLE THOSE CONSONANTS!

In Italian it is important to signal the presence of any double consonants by reinforcing, emphasizing and lengthening the sound.

For instance, if you don't double the consonant in **carro** (*carriage*), you'll end up saying **caro** (*dear*); it's not quite the same! And if you want to say **cappello** (*hat*) but forget to emphasize the double **p**, you will end up saying **capello** (*an individual hair on your head*).

The balance to be struck is a fine one, as some learners, aware of the need to reinforce a double consonant, sometimes go to the other extreme and end up overdoing it!

The same applies to the pronunciation of the rolled **r**: some students go to great lengths to make it audible. The danger is that they end up making quite a roar: *RRRRRRR!* On the other hand, I remember one student telling me that she had an 'oto' at her house in Italy. For a moment I wondered whether she meant a car – could it be a slightly mispronounced version of **automobile**? Then I realized she meant **orto** (*vegetable garden*)! She had simply failed to pronounce the **r**.

DON'T BE TOO ASPIRATIONAL!

Contrary to the English **h**, which is aspirated (produced with a faint but audible emission of air), the Italian **h** is silent; so you should never pronounce words such as **ho** or **hotel** with an audible **h**.

DON'T EAT YOUR VOWELS!

Another pronunciation misdemeanour consists in the tendency to forget that a word contains vowels, and concentrate on saying the consonants instead. One extreme case would be, for instance, to pronounce the name of the town **Ferrara** like this:

f-r-rah ✗

when you should be saying:

fehrrahrah ✓

Even the feminine plural word for *the*, **le**, can be wrongly abbreviated; make sure you fully pronounce the **e** sound: **le** (as in *letter*).

Sometimes the vowels are indeed pronounced, but not quite how they should be. For instance, **Garibaldi** is often mispronounced with the syllable **ba** sounding more like **bo**:

gah-ree-bohl-dee ✗   gah-ree-bahl-dee ✓

3b Say it like you write it

Here are some more sounds which may catch you out if you let yourself be influenced by English or French.

The syllable **au** as in **autobus** and **Australia** is often wrongly pronounced as **o** rather than sounding the two separate vowels:

oh-toh-boos ✘   ah-oo-toh-boos ✔
oh-strah-lee-ah ✘   ah-oo-strah-lee-ah ✔

QU AND GU SOUNDS: SAY THEM LIKE A DUCK!

Any experience of learning French may be responsible for the mispronunciation of **qu** and **gu**. Don't keep them hard, but let the 'u' be heard, as in the English *quick* or *guano*.

qui	keeh ✘	koo-ee ✔
guardare	gahr-dah-reh ✘	goo-ahr-dah-reh ✔
guida	gee-dah ✘	goo-ee-dah ✔
quattordici	ka-ttohr-dee-chee ✘	koo-ah-ttohr-dee-chee ✔

' ah-oo-toh-boos '

'TRASFERIRE' OR 'TRANSFERIRE'?

Many Italian words resemble English ones, for instance:

trasferire ✓ **costruire** ✓
iscriversi ✓ **costituire** ✓
ginnastica ✓

Very frequently, students unwittingly add an **n** when they say these words, because their mother tongue has similar words with an extra **n** or **m**:

traNsferire ✗ **coNstruire** ✗
iNscriversi ✗ **coNstituire** ✗
giMnastica ✗

In the same way, words such as **esperienza, esperto** and **espresso** often acquire an unwelcome **x** in place of the **s**:

eXperienza ✗ **esperienza** ✓
eXperto ✗ **esperto** ✓
eXpresso ✗ **espresso** ✓

'Sono un esperto!'

4 Euro, spaghetti bolognese and **più**, **può**, **poi**

EURO

Euro is one of the most frequently mispronounced words of all time!

Here is how you should say it:
eh-oo-roh ✓

Don't say:
ee-oo-roh ✗

The same applies to other words starting with the letters **eu**, such as **Europa**:
eh-oo-roh-pah ✓
ee-oo-roh-pah ✗

IS IT 'PUB' OR 'POOB'?

Learners may attempt to pronounce English or other foreign words in the 'Italian way', for instance, for **garage** and **routine** they carefully (but wrongly) pronounce the final vowel:

gah-rah-jeh ✗   gh-rah-jh (soft g at the end but no e) ✓
roo-tee-neh ✗   roo-teen ✓ (no e at the end)

For **club** and **pub** they say 'cloob' or 'poob', when in actual fact what Italians say sounds like:

cleh-b (slightly different from English)
pah-b (just the same as in English)

As you can see, Italians do attempt to pronounce foreign words according to the rules of the foreign language concerned, but not always successfully. An interesting case is that of the word **partner**, which Italians pronounce as it is written, including the **r**: 'paRtner', whereas in English the **r** is not sounded. Italians also tend to get the pronunciation of **a** slightly wrong in English imports: **a** often ends up sounding like the Italian **e**, for instance **cat** ends up sounding like 'keht' (as in *kettle*)!

IS IT 'TEHVEH' OR 'TEEVOO'?

When the letters **v** or **w** occur in acronyms or abbreviations, as in **TV** or **www**, they sound like 'voo':

TV = tee-voo
www = voo-voo-voo
BMW = bee-eh-mmeh-voo

WORDS BEGINNING WITH PS

Words such as **psicologo** and **psicanalisi** are pronounced with an audible **ps**, so don't make the mistake of dropping the **p**. What you get is very similar to a hissing sound. Practise this sound by overdoing it slightly: pssss …

SPAGHETTI BOLOGNESE

In English, the letters **gn** produce individual sounds: a hard **g** sound, followed by an **n** – think of *dignity* or *Agnes*. In Italian, these letters merge to form a **ny** sound as in the middle of *onion*. If you know some Spanish, this sound is identical to the **ñ** in *señor*.

agnello	*lamb*	ah-nyeh-llo

'PIÙ' – 'PUÒ' – 'POI' – 'PUOI'

Sometimes students struggle to say these words, puzzled by the combinations of vowels. Practise them, stressing the underlined syllable.

poi	*then/afterwards*	<u>poh</u>-ee
più	*more*	pee-<u>oo</u>
può	*he/she can*	poo-<u>oh</u>
puoi	*you can*	poo-<u>oh</u>-ee
vuoi	*you want*	voo-<u>oh</u>-ee
i miei	*my/mine*	ee mee-<u>eh</u>-ee
i tuoi	*your/yours*	ee too-<u>oh</u>-ee
cui	*that/which*	<u>coo</u>-ee

5 Accent deficit disorder

Consider the spelling of the words underlined in the list below:

giovedi ✗
Mi piace la <u>citta</u> <u>perche</u> <u>e</u> interessante. ✗
<u>ventitre</u> ✗
<u>poverta</u> ✗
<u>opportunita</u> ✗

Each of those words requires an accent to signal where the stress falls: that graphic sign is a necessary part of their spelling. If you leave the accent out, your writing will look a bit careless and can lead to misunderstandings as well as incorrect pronunciation. Here are the correct spellings:

giovedì ✓	*Thursday*
Mi piace la città perché è interessante. ✓	*I like the town because it is interesting.*
ventitrè ✓	*twenty-three*
povertà ✓	*poverty*
opportunità ✓	*opportunity*

Italian accents can either be grave (è) or acute (é). Most words have grave accents and the sounds are pronounced very 'open', but the e in **perché** and **né** has an acute accent and sounds more 'closed'.

Insight
Italians very rarely worry about the direction of their accents when they write, unless they are linguists. Even journalists happily mix up acute and grave accents in their articles without fear of being reprimanded. You can be forgiven for using the wrong accent, but there is no excuse for not using it at all.

One of the most common mistakes is forgetting to use the accent with the verb è (*is*), as opposed to the conjunction e (*and*). This accent is absolutely essential, as the words look and sound the same but have completely different meanings. Compare e and è in these examples:

Il cane <u>e</u> il gatto mangiano.	*The dog <u>and</u> the cat are eating.*
Il cane <u>è</u> stanco.	*The dog <u>is</u> tired.*

The same applies to **ne** and **né**: **ne** is a pronoun that means *of it/ of them* and doesn't take an accent, while **né** means *neither/nor* and does need an accent to signal this different function:

– Quante penne hai?	*How many pens do you have?*
– <u>Ne</u> ho due.	*I have two <u>of them</u>.*
Non ha <u>né</u> fame <u>né</u> sete.	*He is neither hungry nor thirsty.*

The words **lì** and **là**, when they mean *there*, and **sì**, when it means *yes*, also require an accent.

6 Monday, January, English: NO CAPITALS PLEASE!

If you write days of the week, months and nationalities with a capital letter, you are making a mistake (unless of course the word starts a new sentence!).

Lunedi ✗	Aprile ✗	Inglese ✗
lunedì ✓	aprile ✓	inglese ✓

The correct way is to write these words beginning with a lower case letter, as in the lists below.

gennaio	*January*
febbraio	*February*
marzo	*March*
aprile	*April*
maggio	*May*
giugno	*June*
luglio	*July*
agosto	*August*
settembre	*September*
ottobre	*October*
novembre	*November*
dicembre	*December*
lunedì	*Monday*
martedì	*Tuesday*
mercoledì	*Wednesday*
giovedì	*Thursday*
venerdì	*Friday*
sabato	*Saturday*
domenica	*Sunday*
italiano	*Italian*
inglese	*English*
americano	*American*
cinese	*Chinese*
britannico	*British*

The words for nationalities are spelt as listed on page 16 when they refer to the language or a masculine noun. When applied to a feminine noun, those ending in **-o** need to change and end in **-a**:

una città americana *an American town*

The word **io** is written with a lower case i, unlike its equivalent in English, *I*.

Però io non ci vado. *However, I'm not going.*

Questo è il mio ragazzo, Davide. È Italiano.

Vuoi dire che è italiano!

7a Drop the dead vowel

With many of the most common short words (articles, prepositions, pronouns), if they end in a vowel and the word that follows begins with a vowel, a common mistake is to forget to drop the vowel of that first word:

la Italia ✗
la Inghilterra ✗
la amica ✗

Keeping the **a** in **la** in those phrases sounds unnatural and stilted. In order to give a nice flow to the pronunciation, the **a** needs to be dropped and replaced with an apostrophe:

l'Italia ✓   *Italy*
l'Inghilterra ✓   *England*
l'amica ✓   *the friend (female)*

The same applies when **la** is an object pronoun meaning *it* or *her*; and it applies to **lo** meaning *it* or *him*:

La ho comprata. ✗
L'ho comprata. ✓   *I have bought it. (where 'it' is feminine)*
Lo hai comprato? ✗
L'hai comprato?   *Have you bought it? (where 'it' is masculine)*

Remember though that the vowel is <u>not</u> dropped at the end of the equivalent <u>plural</u> words, **le** and **gli** (*the*), or **li** and **le** (*them*):

le amiche	*(female) friends*
gli amici	*(male) friends*
gli inglesi	*the English*
Li ho comprati.	*I have bought them. (masculine)*
Le ho viste.	*I have seen them. (feminine)*

An apostrophe replaces the vowel in the following cases:
▶ with singular articles (**una, la, lo**):

un'amica	*a female friend*
l'amica	*the female friend*
l'amico	*the male friend*

But don't go too far – it's <u>not</u> **un'amico**, because masculine nouns beginning with a vowel stick with **un**:

un amico	*a male friend*

▶ with prepositions (**a, di, in, su**) when they combine with **la** and **lo** to form **alla**, **nella**, etc.:

all'estero	*abroad (m.)*
dell'acqua	*some water*
nell'acqua	*in the water*
sull'acqua	*on the water*

There are more overleaf.

7b Drop the dead vowel

Here are more examples of times when you need to use an apostrophe to replace a vowel:

▶ with singular demonstrative adjectives (**questo, questa, quello, quella**):

quest'uomo	*this man*
quest'affare	*this thing/business*
quell'albero	*that tree*
quell'amica	*that friend*

▶ with the adjectives **bello/a** and **santo/a** when placed in front of the noun:

un bell'uomo	*a handsome man*
sant'Antonio	*St Anthony*

▶ when **come, dove** and **ci** are placed in front of forms of the verb **essere** such as **è, era, erano**:

Com'è andata?	*How did it go?*
C'è Luigi?	*Is Luigi there?*
C'erano troppi turisti.	*There were too many tourists.*
Dov'è?	*Where is he?*

▶ in fixed expressions such as:

senz'altro	*of course*
mezz'ora	*half an hour*

▶ Some verbs such as **dovere, potere, sapere** very often drop the e of the infinitive when followed by another verb:
È importante <u>saper</u> parlare   *It's important to be able to*
una lingua straniera.   *speak a foreign language.*

▶ In some cases, the use of the apostrophe is optional:
Non mi importa./Non m'importa.   *I don't care.*

Notice the common use of this kind of contraction in spoken conversation, though not in writing:

spoken: **Ieri sera ho visto degl'amici.**   *Yesterday I saw some friends.*
written: **Ieri sera ho visto degli amici.**   *Yesterday I saw some friends.*

Insight

Having just talked about vowels that should be dropped, it is also worth mentioning 'linguistic implants' that are inserted when an **e** or an **a** in isolation is followed by a word starting with a vowel.

In some cases it is advisable to 'implant' the letter **d** in between, to get a better, more rounded sound:

**È la lavatrice più cara <u>e è</u> la
   migliore.** ✗
**È la lavatrice più cara <u>ed è</u> la   *It's the most expensive washing
   migliore.** ✓   machine and it's the best.*

<u>A agosto</u> compio 20 anni. ✗
<u>Ad agosto</u> compio 20 anni. ✓   *In August I'll turn 20.*

8 Word liposuction

Consider these phrases:

il signore Bianchi ✗
un buono pranzo ✗

They both contain a very common mistake: the words **signore** and **buono** should have dropped the vowel at the end:

il signor Bianchi ✓
un buon pranzo ✓

Sometimes, a vowel or a whole syllable has to be dropped in front of another word and there is no need to signal this event with an apostrophe as in Chapter 7. This happens with the following adjectives: **grande, bello, santo, quello, buono** which become **gran, bel, san, quel, buon** when they are placed before a <u>masculine</u> noun:

un gran signore	*a real gentleman/a noble man*
un gran finale	*a grand finale*
un bel signore	*a handsome man*
san Giovanni	*St John*
un buon amico	*a good friend*

The same principle applies to **uno, ciascuno** (*each, each one*), **nessuno** (*no, nobody/none*) and **quale** (*what/which*):

un uomo	*a man*
ciascun uomo	*each man*
nessun posto	*nowhere*
nessun problema	*no problem*
Qual è il tuo programma preferito?	*What is your favourite programme?*

By contrast, in the next examples **nessuno** and **ciascuno** are kept in full as they stand alone and are not followed by a noun:

Nessuno lo conosce.   *Nobody knows him.*
Ha dato un regalo a ciascuno   *She gave a gift to each one of us.*
  di noi.

The final -e is also dropped from male titles followed by a first name or surname:

il signore Bianchi ✗	**il signor Bianchi** ✓
il dottore Zivago ✗	**il dottor Zivago** ✓
il signore Aldo ✗	**il signor Aldo** ✓

But sometimes when you drop a whole syllable or a vowel the apostrophe is indeed necessary. This is the case with **po'** (**poco**) and imperatives such as **sta'** (**stai**) and **va'** (**vai**). Notice that both alternatives, full and truncated, are possible:

un po' di pane/un poco di pane   *a bit of bread*
Sta' qui con noi./Stai qui con noi.   *Stay here with us.*
Va' via./Vai via.   *Go away.*

Insight

The trick when trying to decide whether **bello** and **buono** need to be shortened to **bel** and **buon** is to follow the rule for definite and indefinite articles:

il signore = bel signore
un uomo = buon uomo

Nowadays **buon** + word beginning with consonant tends to be the norm, particularly in spoken Italian, e.g. **un buon studente**, even though, strictly speaking, it should be **un buono studente** because **studente** begins with **s** + consonant.

9 Learn to count

A whole raft of mistakes occur with numbers. In general terms, numbers in Italian are straightforward given that, as in English, the higher value precedes the lower one. But numbers up to 19 are irregular and need to be learnt by heart.

Here are some key points to remember.

▶ Beyond 20, when combining with -1 or -8, the 'tens' figure drops the vowel at the end:
  20 venti
  21 ventiuno ✗   21 ventuno ✓
  22 ventidue, 23 ventitré, 24 ventiquattro, etc.
  28 ventiotto ✗   28 ventotto ✓

▶ When giving a date, use a cardinal number, except for the very first day of the month where the ordinal number is used: **primo**

primo maggio ✓	**uno maggio ✗**	*1st May*
secondo maggio ✗	**due maggio ✓**	*2nd May*
terzo maggio ✗	**tre maggio ✓**	*3rd May*

▶ To say *in* a certain year, make sure you use the combined preposition **nel** and not the simple preposition **in**:
  in 2010 ✗   nel 2010 ✓

▶ When you write large numbers out in words, do not split up the words but write it as a long single word:

100.000	**cento mila ✗**	**centomila ✓**
900.000	**nove cento mila ✗**	**novecentomila ✓**

Careful how you write 100 and 1000:

100	**un cento ✗**	**cento ✓**
1000	**un mille ✗**	**mille ✓**

Up to 1999, a thousand is **mille**:
1999   millenovecentonovantanove

From 2000 onwards, use plural thousands, **mila**:
2010   **duemiladieci**

▶ In decimal numbers, an English decimal point becomes an Italian decimal comma – **virgola**:
2.5 = due punto cinque ✗   **2,5 = due virgola cinque** ✓

Just as with the decimal point in English, very large numbers can also be read with a **virgola**:

3,300,000 €	**tre virgola tre millioni di euro**	*3.3 million euros*
3,300,000,000 €	**tre virgola tre miliardi di euro**	*3.3 billion euros*

▶ Prices – to say how much something costs in euros:
Il libro costa sei euro e novantanove.   *The book is €6.99.*

The word **euro** doesn't have a plural form, and the word **centesimi** (*cents*) is usually left out for amounts over one euro. However, for amounts below one euro, you do need to say **centesimi**:
una moneta da dieci centesimi   *a ten-cent coin*

▶ Figures for exchange rates or the shares index use **e** rather than **virgola**:

L'euro vale un dollaro <u>e</u> 41 centesimi.	*The euro is worth $1.41.*
Il FTSE MIB guadagna l'uno <u>e</u> quarantatrè per cento.	*The FTSE MIB has gone up 1.43%.*

▶ Phone numbers are usually read out one figure at a time, except for those which flow better when said in twos or threes:

00 39 02 74852200	**zero zero tre nove zero due sette quattro otto cinque due due zero zero**
800 22 22 1	**ottocento ventidue ventidue uno**

Insight
Never say **doppio** to express a double figure:

88	**doppio otto** ✗	**otto otto** ✓	**ottantotto** ✓

Getting the structure right

See Chapter 30b

10 Strategic positioning of the adverb

Read this statement:

Sempre martedì vado a un corso di salsa. ✗

The speaker unwittingly stressed the word **sempre** by placing it at the beginning of the sentence. If there is no need to highlight an adverb such as **sempre** (*always*), **qualche volta** (*sometimes*), **di solito** (*usually*), put it <u>after</u> the verb, like this:

Il martedì vado <u>sempre</u> a un corso di salsa. ✓	*On Tuesdays I always go to a salsa class.*
Il weekend vado <u>di solito</u> al cinema. ✓	*At the weekend I usually go to the cinema.*

You could emphasize **di solito** or **qualche volta** by placing them at the beginning of the sentence, but not **sempre** as it just doesn't sound right in Italian (except in poetry!).

Di solito il martedì vado a un corso di salsa. Qualche volta vado invece al cinema.	*Usually, on Tuesdays I go to a salsa class. Sometimes I go to the cinema instead.*

Now consider this mistake:

Mi molto piace la primavera. ✗

The speaker has made a common mistake here by assuming that they can translate word for word from the English: *I really like spring.* But in Italian **mi piace** forms an 'unsplittable' item that can't be separated (not even in poetry!). The correct form is therefore:

Mi piace molto la primavera. ✓

The role of the adverb is to better define, or modify, a verb by adding various types of information to it:

Mangio tanto.	*I eat a lot.*
Mangio bene.	*I eat well.*
Mangio tardi.	*I eat late.*
Mangio qui.	*I eat here.*
Mangio lentamente.	*I eat slowly.*

Adverbs can also modify adjectives:

Oggi sono <u>molto stanco</u>.   *Today I am very tired.*

They can modify other adverbs:

Parlava <u>molto lentamente</u>.   *He spoke very slowly.*

Or modify an entire sentence:

<u>Forse</u> andiamo a trovare mia zia   *Perhaps we'll go to see my aunt*
  domenica.   *on Sunday.*

The position of the adverb in the sentence depends on the particular role it plays. If it is to modify an adjective or another adverb, it will usually be placed before them, as illustrated above. If it is to modify the entire phrase, as illustrated by the sentences below, its position can vary, depending on the degree of emphasis we want to place on it:

<u>Forse</u> andiamo a trovare mia zia domenica.   +
Andiamo <u>forse</u> a trovare mia zia domenica.   ++
Andiamo a trovare mia zia domenica, <u>forse</u>.   +++

The position of the adverb in relation to the verb can also vary, depending on what we wish to highlight. If we place the adverb before the verb, we highlight it and give it more prominence. In the case of a compound verb, if we place an adverb in between, this will also serve to highlight it:

Ho <u>rapidamente</u> afferrato le chiavi.   *I quickly picked up the keys.*

11 Use and abuse of **anche**

Anche is an interesting word, in that it does translate as *also* or *too*, but English speakers tend to use it inappropriately, far too often and in the wrong place.

Here are some typical wrong sentences:

Anche devo studiare. ✗
Anche mi sembra che imparo molto su Internet. ✗
Anche ho fatto una bella torta. ✗

The correct version of each sentence is:

Devo anche studiare. ✓	*Also, I have to study.*
Mi sembra anche che imparo molto su Internet. ✓	*It also seems to me that I learn a lot on the internet.*
Ho fatto anche una bella torta. ✓	*I've made a lovely fruit tart too.*
Ho anche fatto una bella torta. ✓	*I've also made a lovely fruit tart.*

If what you mean is *in addition* or *furthermore*, **anche** needs to go in second or third position in the sentence.

If you'd rather put *also* right at the beginning, you need a different word altogether, such as **inoltre**, but be aware that **inoltre** is a bit more formal than **anche**:

Inoltre ho comprato una macchina nuova.	*Also/In addition, I bought a new car.*
Ho anche comprato una macchina nuova.	*I also bought a new car.*

Exceptions to the rule of never placing **anche** at the beginning of the sentence are shown in these examples:

Anche Maria è simpatica.	*Maria too is nice./Maria is nice too.*
Anch'io studio Italiano.	*I too study Italian./I study Italian too.*
Anche i bambini sono andati via.	*The children have gone away too.*
Anche quest'estate andiamo in Italia.	*This summer too we're going to Italy.*

In other words, **anche** can be placed at the beginning of the sentence when it is followed by a name (**Maria**), a subject pronoun (**io**), a noun (**i bambini**) or an expression of time (**quest'estate**), and in a few other specific cases.

Insight

If **anche** is used together with **se** or **quando**, it acquires a different meaning and can then go at the beginning of the sentence:

Anche se sto male, oggi vado a lavorare.	*Even though/Although I'm unwell, today I'm going to work.*
Anche quando sto male, vado a lavorare.	*Even when I'm unwell, I go to work.*

Anche is often followed by **io** and is then abbreviated to **anch'**:

Vengo anch'io.	*I'm coming too.*

'Vengo anch'io.'

12 Was the meal well, good or beautiful?

Consider these phrases and the mistakes they contain:

1 Abbiamo pranzato in un ristorante italiano bene. ✗
2 una persona molto bene ✗
3 Abito in una città bene. ✗
4 un benissimo pranzo ✗
5 un film bene ✗

It's essential to keep **bene** as an adverb (meaning *well*) and not attempt to apply it to nouns: choose one of a whole range of adjectives instead, as in the correct models below.

1 Abbiamo pranzato in un <u>buon</u> ristorante italiano. ✓	*We had lunch in a good Italian restaurant.*
2 un'<u>ottima</u> persona/una <u>brava</u> persona ✓	*a very good person/a good person*
3 Abito in una <u>bella</u> città. ✓	*I live in a nice town.*
4 un <u>buonissimo</u> pranzo ✓	*an excellent meal*
5 un <u>buon</u> film ✓	*a good movie*

A variation on this error is to confuse **bene** and **molto**:

Questi colori mi piacciono bene. ✗
Questi colori mi piacciono molto. ✓   *I like these colours very much.*

Another family of words with potential for error is the adjective **bello** in all its forms. In Italian, a nice meal should not be described as bellissimo! Only **buono** or **buonissimo** are normally used to make a positive comment on the taste of food. The exception to this is when people say something like this:

Ho mangiato un bel piatto di pasta.	*I ate/I've eaten a nice plate of pasta.*
Oggi mia moglie cucina delle belle lasagne al forno.	*Today my wife is cooking some nice lasagne.*

But they would absolutely never say:

Ho mangiato un piatto di pasta molto bello. ✗
Oggi mia moglie cucina delle lasagne molto belle. ✗

In other words, use **bello** with caution when describing food. If you do use it, you will be emphasizing your emotional involvement in the experience and not just the food itself. Remember that **bello** in that case will have to go before the noun.

un piatto di spaghetti bello ✗
un bel piatto di spaghetti ✓

È proprio un bellissimo piatto di spaghetti!

Here are some more examples of correct usage of **bello**, unrelated to food:

un tramonto bellissimo	*a very beautiful sunset*
una bella donna	*a beautiful woman*
una canzone bellissima	*a very beautiful song*

As you have noticed, **bello** can go before as well as after the noun: more on that in Chapter 26.

Bello is an adjective and changes its form depending on the word it qualifies. On the other hand, **bene** and **benissimo** are adverbs and don't change.

Stai bene?	*Are you well/ok?*
Canta bene.	*He sings well.*
Va tutto bene?	*Is everything ok?*
Le cose vanno benissimo.	*Things are going really well.*

Insight

Notice in the last two examples the use of the verb **andare** (**va/vanno**) instead of the verb **essere** (**è/sono**), to say *Is everything ok?* and *Things <u>are</u> going really well.*

13 Compare and contrast

In comparative sentences, students often end up using the wrong word, in particular by mixing **che** and **di**:

Maria è più alta che Carlo. ✗
Maria è più alta di Carlo. ✓   *Maria is taller than Carlo.*

As a general rule, if you are comparing like for like, i.e. items belonging to the same categories, use **di**:

**Il gatto è più indipendente che
il cane.** ✗
Il gatto è più indipendente del   *Cats are more independent*
cane. ✓   *than dogs.*

You also need to use **di** with numbers:

Mia nonna ha più di novant'anni.   *My grandmother is more than
90 years old.*

You need to use **di** with names and with pronouns such as **me, lui, lei, noi** (*me, him, her, us*):

Carla gioca meglio di Maria.   *Carla plays better than Maria.*
Hanno meno soldi di noi.   *They have less money than
we do.*

Use **che** instead of **di** in the following situations:

▶ when comparing infinitives:
    Giocare a tennis è più faticoso   *Playing tennis is more tiring*
    che camminare.   *than walking.*
    Andare in aereo è più veloce   *Going by plane is quicker*
    che andare in treno.   *than going by train.*

- when comparing two adjectives referring to the same thing or person:

Adriano è più intelligente che bello.   *Adriano is more intelligent than handsome.*

Siamo più affamati che stanchi.   *We are more hungry than tired.*

- before a preposition:

È più rapido andare in aereo che in treno.   *It's quicker to go by plane than by train.*

È meno caro fare la spesa al supermercato che nel negozio vicino casa.   *It's cheaper to shop at the supermarket than in the shop near home.*

Insight

Bear in mind that in colloquial Italian and in some dialects, the boundaries between **che** and **di** are occasionally blurred. Nonetheless, try to stick to it, particularly in writing and in a formal context.

'Serena è più giovane di Martina.'

14 Don't go over the top!

Consider this sentence:

È un'attrice molto bellissima. ✗

It is wrong because **bellissima** is an 'absolute superlative' – you can't add **molto** to it. It can't be qualified any further, as it already expresses a quality to the highest possible degree.

The correct form of the sentence is:

È un'attrice bellissima. ✓   *She's a really beautiful actress.*

Bellissimo/buonissimo and other words ending in **-issimo**, as well as **squisito, fantastico, splendido, eccellente, meraviglioso** are absolute superlatives and cannot be preceded by **molto, poco** and so on; they do not require further qualification.

The tables below list irregular comparatives and superlatives.

adjective	comparative	superlative
buono	**migliore**	**buonissimo/ottimo**
good	*better*	*very good/excellent*
cattivo	**peggiore**	**pessimo**
bad	*worse*	*worst*

adverb	comparative	superlative
bene	**meglio**	**benissimo**
well	*better*	*very well*

Insight

You can form the absolute superlative of other adjectives or adverbs by dropping the vowel at the end of the word and adding -issimo or by placing **molto** or **tanto** in front of it:

1 **un bambino molto bravo**
2 **un bambino tanto bravo**
3 **un bambino bravissimo**

All those sentences mean *a very good child*, but the tone is increasingly emphatic as we progress from number 1 to number 3.

'buono ...

... migliore ...

... buonissimo!'

15 Learn to do without di

Everyone gets prepositions wrong when they're learning Italian, but you could make your life considerably easier by just cutting them out when they aren't necessary!

Consider this sentence:

È normale di fare errori quando si impara una lingua. ✗

And now consider this one:

È normale fare errori quando si impara una lingua. ✓
It is normal to make mistakes when learning a language.

It is wrong to add **di** in impersonal sentences like this, i.e. sentences without a subject. No preposition is required when you are making general statements beginning *it is* or *it was*, as in *it is better/ important/essential/nice/bad/useful/advisable to do ...*

È facile imparare l'italiano.
It's easy to learn Italian.

È meglio andare a casa adesso.
It's best to go home now.

È importante avere un sistema di tassazione equo.
It's important to have a fair tax system.

È stato molto interessante visitare posti che avevo visto solo in TV.
It has been very interesting to visit places that I had only seen on TV.

(This type of mistake is probably due to French interference, where the preposition *de* is indeed required to make general statements beginning *il est difficile de .../c'est simple de ...* and so on.)

Try to resist the urge to use **di** in phrases like this:

Trovo molto difficile di imparare il cinese. ✗

Trovo molto difficile imparare il cinese. ✓   *I find it very difficult to learn Chinese.*

In fact that whole construction sounds too much like a literal translation from English and therefore a bit unnatural. Italians are more likely to put it another way, for instance:

Il cinese mi sembra molto difficile.
Faccio molta difficoltà a imparare il cinese.
Il cinese lo trovo molto difficile da imparare.

VERB + 'DI' + INFINITIVE

There are many verbs that do require the preposition **di** to link them to another verb in the infinitive. These include: **augurare, cercare, chiedere, decidere, dimenticare, dire, pensare, sperare.**

Ti auguro di rimetterti presto.   *I hope that you will get better soon.*

Cerchiamo di finire questo lavoro prima possibile.   *Let's try to finish this job as soon as possible.*

Chiedigli di stare zitto.   *Ask him to be quiet.*

Abbiamo deciso di andare a vivere a Roma.   *We've decided to go and live in Rome.*

Laura dimentica sempre di chiudere la porta.   *Laura always forgets to close the door.*

Franco ha detto di aspettarlo nel bar.   *Franco said to wait for him at the bar.*

Penso di invitare anche Lorenzo.   *I am thinking of inviting Lorenzo too.*

Speriamo di vincere la partita.   *We're hoping to win the match.*

16 Is it 'on' Monday?

Remember not to translate literally *on Monday/Tuesday/etc.*
Students come up with all sorts of inventive ways to translate that
little word *on*. For instance, for *I'm going to the cinema on Friday*,
they might say:

Vado al cinema <u>a</u> venerdì. ✗
Vado al cinema <u>sul</u> venerdì. ✗

This is wrong as *on* should not be translated at all!

Vado al cinema venerdì. ✓

If you want to convey the fact that you do something on a regular
basis, for example, to say that you go to the cinema <u>on Fridays</u> or
<u>every Friday</u>, then all you need is the definite article:

Vado al cinema <u>il</u> venerdì. ✓	*I go to the cinema on Fridays.*
<u>La</u> domenica mi alzo tardi. ✓	*On Sundays I get up late.*
<u>Il</u> sabato mattina vado in palestra.	*On Saturday morning(s) I go to the gym.*
Vado in piscina tutti <u>i</u> fine settimana. ✓	*I go to the swimming pool every weekend.*

Remember, it's **il** for days of the week, which are masculine, except
Sunday: **<u>la</u> domenica**.

Try to memorize the following expressions:

di mattina/la mattina	*in the morning*
di giorno/il giorno	*in the day*
di pomeriggio/nel pomeriggio/il pomeriggio	*in the afternoon*
di sera/la sera	*in the evening*
di notte/la notte	*at night*

Torno a notte. ✗
Torno di notte. ✓   *I'll be back late at night./I get back late*
                              at night.
A notte non dormo. ✗
La notte non dormo. ✓   *I don't sleep at night.*

The preposition *on* tends to generate other types of mistakes, for instance *on the floor*, *on holiday*, *on TV* are often wrongly translated literally when what you need is a different word:

L'appartamento è sul terzo piano. ✗
L'appartamento è <u>al</u> terzo piano. ✓   *The flat is on the third floor.*

**Sulla vacanza porto con me il
   computer.** ✗
**<u>In</u> vacanza porto con me il   *On holiday I take my
   computer.** ✓   computer with me.*

Ho sentito le notizie sulla TV. ✗
Ho sentito le notizie <u>in</u> TV. ✓   *I heard the news on TV.*

It is also important to remember that when you have a preposition (**a, in, su, di**) followed by a word for *the*, these two words have to be joined together.

Vado in banca in il pomeriggio. ✗
Vado in banca <u>nel</u> pomeriggio. ✓   *I'll go to the bank in the
                                                         afternoon.*

C'è un gatto su la tavola. ✗
C'è un gatto <u>sulla</u> tavola. ✓   *There's a cat on the table.*

Mangiamo le verdure di l'orto. ✗
Mangiamo le verdure <u>dell'</u>orto. ✓   *We eat vegetables from the
                                                         garden.*

17 Keep your subjects under control

Overuse of the subject pronoun is rife amongst students, and mostly totally unnecessary! Here are two examples where the pronoun should have been left out:

1 **Nel tempo libero <u>io</u> non mi piace stare in casa. <u>Io</u> di solito faccio sport.** ✗
2 **Quando <u>io</u> sono arrivata a casa, mio marito ha aperto una bottiglia di vino rosso. <u>Lui</u> aveva preparato una cena deliziosa.** ✗

And here is how they should be:

1 **Nel tempo libero non mi piace stare in casa. Di solito faccio sport.** ✓
   In my free time, I don't like staying at home. Usually I do sport.
2 **Quando sono arrivata a casa, mio marito ha aperto una bottiglia di vino rosso. Aveva preparato una cena deliziosa.** ✓
   When I arrived home, my husband opened a bottle of red wine. He had prepared a delicious dinner.

Sentences like these might look fine to English speakers. They are so used to adding the personal pronoun in front of the verb that, however often they might be told to leave it out in Italian, they are reluctant to do so as it feels uncomfortable, as if something important was missing. It is of course a matter of changing an ingrained automatic habit. (Some students also tell me that putting **io/tu/lui** before the verb during a conversation helps them 'buy time' and work out what verb form they are going to need.)

At the risk of repeating myself, I'll say again that in Italian the subject pronoun is left out, as the information provided by the verb is in most cases sufficient to communicate the number and gender of the subject. If I say **balliamo** (*let's dance*) to a native speaker, they will instantly associate **balliamo** with **noi**, because only **noi** uses the verb ending -iamo. Therefore adding **noi** is unnecessary.

Subject pronouns such as **noi** are to be used only for emphasis, to establish a contrast, or when a pronoun stands alone in the sentence:

▶ Emphasis:
   Lo facciamo <u>noi</u>.   *<u>We</u>'ll do it.*
   Vieni anche <u>tu</u> al cinema?   *Are <u>you</u> coming to the cinema too?*

▶ Contrast:
   <u>Io</u> lavoro mentre <u>tu</u> ti diverti.   *<u>I</u> am working while <u>you</u> are*
                                       enjoying yourself.

   <u>Io</u> pago la cena stasera,   *<u>I</u> will pay for dinner tonight,*
     <u>tu</u> paghi la prossima volta.   *<u>you</u> pay next time.*

▶ Pronoun in isolation:
   – Chi è? – Siamo <u>noi</u>.   *– Who's that? – It's us.*

Here is a reminder of the main subject pronouns:

io	*I*	**lei**	*you (formal)*
tu	*you (informal/singular)*	**noi**	*we*
lui	*he*	**voi**	*you (plural)*
lei	*she*	**loro**	*they*

Insight

Occasionally the subject pronoun is left out when actually it should be there. Here is a good example, taken from the beginning of a letter:

Ciao Alex, come stai? Sto bene. ✗
Ciao Alex, come stai? Io sto bene. ✓

If you write *How are you?* and follow it immediately with *I am well*, you should add the pronoun **io** to make the point that, once you've asked your friend how he is, you are now switching and talking about yourself: having asked about <u>you</u>, I'm now letting you know that <u>I</u> am well.

18a Don't be direct with your indirect pronouns

Consider this sentence:

Lo telefono domani. ✗

This sentence is wrong because **lo** is a direct object pronoun and the verb **telefonare** requires an indirect object pronoun, one implying a sense of 'to' or 'at'. The right version is:

Gli telefono domani. ✓   *I'll phone him tomorrow.*

The incorrect use of direct and indirect pronouns is by far one of the most common mistakes among learners; it is usually due to the difficulty of knowing which verb requires a direct or indirect pronoun. Things are further complicated by the fact that some verbs can take both. There is no easy way out. If you read or listen to a lot of Italian, eventually the right pronoun will come to you automatically. In the meantime, check verbs in a good grammar book that gives plenty of examples of how to use them.

Here's an explanation to help you match up verbs with the right object pronouns. Verbs like *take*, *eat*, *visit* – **prendere, mangiare, visitare** – can have a direct reply to questions about *who* or *what*:

Che cosa prendi?   *What will you have?*
Prendo un caffè.   *I'll have a coffee.*

To use these verbs with a pronoun instead of that noun (**caffè**), you need a <u>direct</u> object pronoun:

<u>**Lo**</u> **prendo.**   *I'll have <u>it</u>.*

Verbs like *give*, *explain*, *telephone* – **dare, spiegare, telefonare** – bring a word for *to* or *at* into their reply to questions about *who* or *what*. When stating <u>who</u> you are giving something <u>to</u> (or explaining something to, or telephoning), then you are using a preposition (in Italian, usually **a**):

Telefono a Carla domani.   *I'll phone (to) Carla tomorrow.*

To use these verbs with a pronoun instead of that noun (**Carla**), you need an <u>indirect</u> object pronoun.

<u>Le</u> telefono domani.   *I'll phone <u>her</u> tomorrow.*

Another option, if we need to stress the word *her* for any reason, is to use **lei**:

Telefono a lei.   *It's <u>her</u> that I'm phoning.*

– **lei** is a stressed or emphatic pronoun. Note that **lei** goes after the verb, and that the preposition **a** could equally be replaced by other prepositions such as **con** (*with*) or **per** (*for*).

Now, in the next example, the verb **dare** has two objects, one direct (**un regalo**) and one indirect (**mamma**):

Do un regalo a mamma.   *I give a present to my mum.*

You can replace **un regalo** with a <u>direct object pronoun</u>:

<u>Lo</u> do a mamma.   *I give <u>it</u> to my mum.*

Equally, you can replace **mamma** with an <u>indirect object pronoun</u>:

<u>Le</u> do un regalo.   *I give <u>her</u> a present.*

Take care especially with the Italian words for *him, her, it, them, to him, to her, to it, to them*, since these are easily mixed up. See the table on page 46.

18b Don't be direct with your indirect pronouns

In 18a we saw that if you don't know the difference between direct and indirect object pronouns you could confuse people. So here's a table of them, with the emphatic or stressed pronouns too, for good measure.

	object pronouns		
	direct	indirect	stressed/emphatic
me	mi	mi	a me
you	ti	ti	a te
him	lo	gli	a lui
her	la	le	a lei
you (formal)	la	le	a lei
us	ci	ci	a noi
you (plural)	vi	vi	a voi
them (masculine)	li	gli/loro	a loro
them (feminine)	le	gli/loro	a loro

WHERE TO PUT YOUR PRONOUNS

The unstressed pronouns (direct and indirect) go before the verb (example 1 below) except when the verb is an imperative (2), an infinitive (3) or an '-ing' verb (4):

1	**Lo studio.**	*I study it.*
2	**Studialo!**	*Study it!*
3	**studiarlo**	*to study it*
4	**studiandolo**	*studying it*

'GLI' AND 'LORO'

The difference between the plural forms **gli** and **loro** shown at the end of the table is as follows: **loro** goes after the verb and is formal, whereas **gli** goes before the verb and is mostly used in spoken Italian.

– Cosa hai regalato ai tuoi genitori?
– <u>Gli</u> ho regalato una televisione nuova.
– What did you give as a present to your parents?
– I gave them a new television.

L'impiegato ha spiegato <u>loro</u> che il reclamo andava inviato entro otto giorni.
The clerk explained to them that the complaint had to be sent within eight days.

Insight

Don't forget that the formal *you* translates as **la** if the pronoun is direct and **le** if it is indirect, irrespective of gender:

Signore, <u>la</u> posso aiutare?	*Can I help you, sir?*
Signora, <u>la</u> posso aiutare?	*Can I help you, madam?*
Va bene signore, <u>le</u> telefono domani.	*That's fine, sir, I'll ring you tomorrow.*
Va bene signora, <u>le</u> telefono domani.	*That's fine, madam, I'll ring you tomorrow.*

'Studialo!'

19 Quel or quello? Demonstrate your point!

One common mistake consists of mixing up demonstrative pronouns and demonstrative adjectives.

An example of a demonstrative adjective is _that_ dog; the demonstrative pronoun in this case would be _that one_.

Let me remind you that a pronoun replaces a word, whereas an adjective qualifies a word and therefore accompanies it:

that dog = **quel cane**	– demonstrative adjective
that one = **quello**	– demonstrative pronoun

A common mistake would be to say:

quello cane ✗

... using the pronoun **quello** instead of the adjective **quel**:

quel cane ✓   _that dog_

For a masculine noun, the word for _that_ is **quel, quello** or **quell'** when used just before the noun, or **quello** when it stands alone.

For feminine words, there is no difference between demonstrative adjectives and pronouns:

that house = **quella casa** – demonstrative adjective
that island = **quell'isola** – demonstrative adjective (**quella** is shortened before a vowel)
that one = **quella** – demonstrative pronoun

those houses = **quelle case** – demonstrative adjective
those islands = **quelle isole** – demonstrative adjective
those ones = **quelle** – demonstrative pronoun

	demonstrative adjectives	*demonstrative pronouns*
this (m.)	**questo**	**questo**
this (f.)	**questa**	**questa**
these (m. pl.)	**questi**	**questi**
these (f. pl.)	**queste**	**queste**
that (m.)	**quel**	**quello**
that (m.)	**quello**	**quello**
that (m. before vowel)	**quell'**	**quello**
that (f.)	**quella**	**quella**
that (f. before vowel)	**quell'**	**quella**
those (m. pl.)	**quei**	**quelli**
those (m. pl.)	**quegli**	**quelli**
those (f. pl.)	**quelle**	**quelle**

Insight

The three masculine forms of the demonstrative <u>adjectives</u> have similar endings to the corresponding words for *the*:

quel cane	**il cane**
quello studente	**lo studente**
quell'albero	**l'albero**
quei cani	**i cani**
quegli studenti	**gli studenti**
quegli alberi	**gli alberi**

In other words, the demonstrative adjective ends in the same way as the definite article that would be used with that noun. You will find it easier to get it right if you make sure you know all the forms of the definite article first – see *Chapter 21*!

Quali scarpe vuole provare?

Quelle.

20 Che: the big forgotten one

Consider these sentences:

La prima volta sono andato in Italia era nel 1980. ✗
Ogni volta vado a Roma vedo qualcosa di diverso. ✗

In both sentences an essential word, **che**, has been left out.

La prima volta <u>che</u> sono andato in Italia era nel 1980. ✓
Ogni volta <u>che</u> vado a Roma vedo qualcosa di diverso. ✓

In English you can choose whether to leave out the equivalent of
che (*that/which/who/whom*) or include it in the sentence:
The first time I went to Italy was in 1980.
The first time <u>that</u> I went to Italy was in 1980.
Every time I go to Rome I see something different.
Every time <u>that</u> I go to Rome I see something different.

This is not possible in Italian. **Che** can <u>never</u> be left out. Here is
another example:

Come si chiama la donna che   *What's the name of the woman*
  hai salutato?   *(that) you waved at?*

One of the functions of **che** is to link two phrases together,
replacing a word that would otherwise be repeated. In this case,
it is called a relative pronoun.

Leggo un giornale. Il giornale è molto interessante.
Leggo un giornale <u>che</u> è molto interessante.
I'm reading a newspaper. The newspaper is very interesting.
I'm reading a newspaper which/that is very interesting.

Il ragazzo sta parlando. Si chiama Giorgio.
Il ragazzo <u>che</u> sta parlando si chiama Giorgio.
The boy is talking. He's called Giorgio.
The boy who is talking is called Giorgio.

There are other relative pronouns in addition to **che**, all meaning *that/which/who/whom*:

cui
il quale   **la quale**   **i quali**   **le quali**

Use **cui** instead of **che** whenever the verb requires a preposition. The next two examples both contain the verb **parlare di** (*to speak/talk/tell about*):

La casa <u>di cui</u> ti ho parlato è in vendita.
The house about which I told you is up for sale./The house I told you about is up for sale.

Questo è il libro <u>di cui</u> ti parlavo.
This is the book that I was telling you about.

The relative pronoun **il quale** (and its masculine/feminine/singular/plural permutations) is also used instead of **che** or **cui**, but in colloquial language you won't hear it very often. In written language it is mostly used after a preposition:

Ecco il modulo <u>con il quale</u> può presentare domanda.
Here is the form with which you can apply.

21a The definite article: one in English, six in Italian

Students are forever getting definite articles (*the* in English) wrong. This is not surprising as in English there is only one definite article, as opposed to six in Italian, and the one you need will depend on gender, number, and how the next word begins.

Here are all the options; they may look like more than six, but **l'** is an abbreviation of **lo** or **la** so doesn't count as a separate word.

masculine singular:	**il**	**lo**	**l'**
masculine plural:	**i**	**gli**	
feminine singular:	**la**		**l'**
feminine plural:	**le**		

If a masculine word begins with a consonant, you will need **il** for singular and **i** for plural:

il libro	*the book*
i libri	*the books*
il ragazzo	*the boy*
i ragazzi	*the boys*

If a masculine word begins with any of the letters listed below, you will need **lo**, or its equivalent plural **gli**:

s + consonant	**lo studente**	*the student*
	gli studenti	*the students*
ps	**lo psicologo**	*the psychologist*
gn	**lo gnomo**	*the gnome*
x	**lo xilofono**	*the xylophone*
y	**lo yogurt**	*the yoghurt*
z	**lo zio**	*the uncle*

If a masculine or feminine word begins with a vowel, you will need **l'** (a contraction of **lo** or **la**) for the singular, and **gli** or **le** for the plural:

l'amico	the friend (m.)
gli amici	the friends (m. or m. & f. mixed)
l'amica	the friend (f.)
le amiche	the friends (f.)

Feminine words that begin with a consonant are the most straightforward of all – you need **la** for the singular and **le** for the plural:

| la ragazza | the girl |
| le ragazze | the girls |

One point that can seem odd for learners of Italian is that a mixed group of both masculine and feminine people or things is taken (grammatically) to be masculine. So if you combine **ragazzi** (*boys*) and **ragazze** (*girls*), you call the group **ragazzi** and use the masculine plural word for *the*, **i ragazzi**.

Conversely, when you hear or read **i ragazzi**, it could mean *boys* or *boys and girls* or *young people*. Similarly, **i miei fratelli** could be translated as *my brothers* or, equally, *my brothers and sisters*.

The same kind of mixed-gender translation applies to other words for people: **amici, cugini, figli, insegnanti, nonni, nipoti** – so that you will need to use the context to grasp the intended meaning.

Mia sorella ha tre figli. Si chiamano Francesca, Luigi e Paola.

*My sister has three children. They are called Francesca, Luigi and Paola. (– in this case, **figli** clearly means not just sons but children or sons and daughters)*

Giovanna e Riccardo sono i nipoti di mia madre.

Giovanna and Riccardo are my mother's niece and nephew.

21b The definite article: one in English, six in Italian

It's important to know when you should use a definite article as opposed to when you should leave it out.

Consider these sentences:

Durante il tempo libero guardo TV. ✗
Durante il tempo libero guardo la TV. ✓ *In my free time I watch TV.*

The first sentence is incorrect because the article has been left out.

In Italian, the definite article is necessary in all the cases listed below.

▶ When making general statements or talking about categories:
Gli inglesi bevono molto tè. *The English drink lots of tea.*
I bambini sono vivaci. *Children are lively.*
Adoro gli animali. *I love animals.*

▶ With words denoting objects of frequent use:
Hanno la lavastoviglie. *They have a dishwasher.*

▶ With names of countries:
la Francia *France*
l'Italia *Italy*
gli Stati Uniti *the United States*

▶ With days of the week, to express an event that occurs regularly or habitually (as explained in Chapter 16):
Veniva sempre il venerdì. *He always used to come on Fridays.*

▶ With dates and years:
Il due agosto vado in vacanza. *On the second of August, I'm going on holiday.*

Il 2009 è stato un anno memorabile. *2009 was a memorable year.*

▶ With parts of the body or objects that clearly belong to you:

Ha **la** barba.	*He has a beard.*
Ho **le** mani fredde.	*My hands are cold.*
Si è tagliata **i** capelli.	*She had her hair cut.*
Ho dimenticato **gli** occhiali a casa.	*I've left my glasses at home.*
Ho portato **la** macchina in officina.	*I took my car to the garage.*

▶ With weather features:

La nebbia rallenta la circolazione stradale.	*Fog slows road traffic down.*
Non mi piace **la** pioggia.	*I don't like rain.*

▶ With possessive adjectives (but see Chapter 25 for exceptions):

Ieri ho visto **il** mio professore di matematica.	*Yesterday I saw my maths teacher.*

Do not use the definite article as part of the first line of an address beginning with **via** (*road/street*), **viale** (*avenue*), or **corso** (*high street*):

la via Nazionale n.5 ✗
via Nazionale n.5 ✓

La banca si trova nel corso Umberto, numero 130. ✗	
La banca si trova in corso Umberto, numero 130. ✓	*The bank is at 130 Corso Umberto.*

Insight

The article can be left out in front of possessive pronouns or it can be included for emphasis:

– Di chi è questa penna?	*Whose pen is this?*
– È mia.	*It's mine.*
– È **la** mia.	*It's mine. (more emphatic)*

22a The rules of plurality

Consider these sentences:

Ho dimenticato le chiave a casa. ✗
Avete fatto i compito, bravi! ✗

Both of them contain a mistake relating to the plural. The plural of **la chiave** (*key*) is **le chiavi** (*keys*), and the plural of **il compito** (*homework*) is **i compiti**. So the correct versions are:

Ho dimenticato <u>le chiavi</u> a casa. ✓   *I left my keys at home.*

Avete fatto <u>i compiti</u>, bravi! ✓   *You've done the homework, well done!*

Here is how plural nouns are formed:

NOUNS ENDING IN -A

Nouns ending in **-a** are mostly feminine, and their plural ends in **-e**:

la sorella *sister*	**le sorelle** *sisters*
la casa *house*	**le case** *houses*
la scarpa *shoe*	**le scarpe** *shoes*

But a few nouns that end in **-a** are masculine and their plural ends in **-i**:

il poeta *poet*	**i poeti** *poets*
il problema *problem*	**i problemi** *problems*
il teorema *theorem*	**i teoremi** *theorems*
il programma *programme*	**i programmi** *programmes*
il socialista *socialist*	**i socialisti** *socialists*

Note: words such as **problema** and **teorema** come from Greek and have retained the same gender they had in that language.

NOUNS ENDING IN -O

Nouns ending in -o are mostly masculine and their plural ends in -i:

il ragazzo *boy*	**i ragazzi** *boys*
l'effetto *effect*	**gli effetti** *effects*

But several nouns ending in -o have an irregular plural:

il labbro *lip (m.)*	**le labbra** *lips (f.)*
il lenzuolo *sheet (m.)*	**le lenzuola** *sheets (f.)*
l'uovo *egg (m.)*	**le uova** *eggs (f.)*
la mano *hand (f.)*	**le mani** *hands (f.)*

NOUNS ENDING IN -E

Nouns ending in -e can be either masculine or feminine, and their plural ends in -i. So plurals ending in -i are not all masculine.

il padre *father*	**i padri** *fathers*
il pallone *football*	**i palloni** *footballs*
la madre *mother*	**le madri** *mothers*
la ragione *reason*	**le ragioni** *reasons*
la chiave *key*	**le chiavi** *keys*

Insight

The plural of many common words ending in -co or -ca requires an additional **h** before the final **i** or **e**, in order to preserve the same 'hard' sound:

il fuoco	i fuochi
il turco	i turchi
l'amica	le amiche
la banca	le banche
la discoteca	le discoteche

Similarly, many words ending in -go or -ga need to add an **h** in the plural, to keep the hard **g** sound:

il sugo	i sughi
il/la collega	i colleghi/le colleghe

22b The rules of plurality

UNCHANGING PLURALS

Some nouns are identical in the singular and the plural.
To determine whether they are singular or plural, it is necessary
to look at the other words placed beside them, or the context in
which they are used.

il cinema *cinema*	**i cinema** *cinemas*
il re *king*	**i re** *kings*
la radio *radio*	**le radio** *radios*

Similarly, foreign words are usually left unchanged in the plural:

il film	**i film**
il caffè	**i caffè**
il weekend	**i weekend**

Nouns ending in an accented vowel are also unchanged in the plural:

la città *town*	**le città** *towns*
una possibilità *one possibility*	**molte possibilità** *many possibilities*

UNCOUNTABLE NOUNS

Some nouns, described as 'uncountable', are mainly used in their
singular form, as in English:

il latte	*milk*
il vino	*wine*
l'acqua	*water*
il riso	*rice*
la frutta	*fruit*
l'aria	*air*
l'ossigeno	*oxygen*

If they are turned into plurals, their meaning changes slightly:

Ho comprato due ottimi vini.	*I've bought two excellent types of wine.*

The word **frutta** (*fruit*) is normally singular and feminine, but a masculine plural version **frutti** is found in some fixed expressions:

Mangio molta frutta ogni giorno.	*I eat a lot of fruit every day.*
frutti di bosco	*wild berries*
frutti di mare	*seafood*
raccogliere i frutti del proprio lavoro	*to reap the fruits of one's labour*

THERE'S NO SUCH THING AS A SCISSOR!

There are also nouns used only or mainly in the plural:

le forbici	*scissors*
le dimissioni	*resignation*
le ferie	*time off work/holiday*
i pantaloni	*trousers*

Note that for the last item in that list, the singular form **il pantalone** does exist, but it isn't used very frequently. In most contexts, it's safer to call them **pantaloni**.

Non riesco a trovare le forbici.	*I can't find the scissors.*
Ho deciso di dare le dimissioni.	*I've decided to resign.*
Quando hai le ferie?	*When do you go on holiday?*
Questi pantaloni mi stanno stretti.	*These trousers feel tight.*

23 Some people are singular

English speakers tend to be flexible about whether nouns used to talk about two or more people or things (such as *staff*, *people*, *police*) should be treated as singular or plural. Italian speakers are more strict on this point and collective nouns are seen as singular. In the same way, nouns preceded by the words for *some*, *each*, *every* are also seen as singular.

'QUALCHE'

One frequent translation for *some* is **qualche**. When using this word, students almost invariably assume that it must be followed by a plural, as in English. This is a mistake, as **qualche** is always followed by a singular word:

Vorrei comprare qualche riviste. ✗
Vorrei comprare qualche <u>rivista</u>. ✓   *I'd like to buy some magazines.*

Insight

Similar to **qualche** is the word **ogni**, meaning *each* or *every*. Students assume that **ogni** has to be followed by a plural noun, owing to the fact that it looks plural because it ends in **i**. The spelling is misleading.

ogni studente	*each student*
ogni persona	*each person*
Controllo la posta elettronica ogni giorno.	*I check my emails every day.*

'LA GENTE'

A similar problem applies to *people*. It is rightly translated as **gente**, but please remember that this word is singular in Italian and needs singular (feminine) forms to go with it:

<u>Tutta la gente</u> con cui lavoro <u>è</u> molto <u>simpatica</u>.   *All the people I work with <u>are</u> very nice.*

The same principle applies to other words which convey the idea of two or more people: *couple, group, police, staff, personnel, team, family, cabinet, government.* In Italian these words are always singular, while in English they can be either singular or plural:

La polizia sta facendo un ottimo lavoro. *(singular)*
The police is doing a great job. (singular)
The police are doing a great job. (plural)

È proprio una bella coppia. *They make a lovely couple.*
Il personale sciopererà dalle *The staff will be on strike from*
11 alle 15. *11 am to 3 pm.*

'LA PASTA E GLI SPAGHETTI'

Pasta is a collective noun and is singular, except when it means *a pastry*, in which case it has both singular and plural forms, or when it describes different sorts of pasta: **le paste lunghe/corte/fresche** *long/short/fresh types of pasta*. By contrast, **spaghetti**, **tortellini**, and all the other types of pasta are plural:

La pasta che hai cucinato è *The pasta you cooked is very good.*
molto buona.
Vorrei due paste al cioccolato. *I'd like two chocolate pastries.*
Per pranzo cucino gli spaghetti *For lunch I'm cooking spaghetti*
al pomodoro. *with tomato sauce.*

Lasagne, on the other hand, can be singular as well as plural:

un'ottima lasagna *an excellent lasagna*
delle ottime lasagne *some excellent lasagne*

Sai fare la lasagna con la salsa *Can you cook white sauce*
bianca? *lasagne?*
Oggi mamma ha cotto le *Today my mum has cooked*
lasagne al forno. *baked lasagne.*

24 The gender of the problem

Consider these words:

la fine settimana ✗   **la clima ✗**   **il tradizione ✗**

What is wrong in each case is the definite article, and the mistake arises from getting the gender of the noun wrong. Here are the right forms:

il fine settimana ✓   **il clima ✓**   **la tradizione ✓**

Note that *the end* is a feminine word, **la fine,** but *the weekend* is masculine: **il fine settimana,** or alternatively **il weekend.** This is because **fine settimana** derives from English, and foreign words are by and large masculine.

In Italian the gender of a noun is either masculine or feminine. This grammatical difference does not always reflect the actual gender of a person; for instance **il soprano** is a masculine word even though it usually refers to a female singer.

The gender of a word can usually be determined by looking at its ending. There are three main categories:

NOUNS ENDING IN -A

These are mainly **feminine** nouns, like these examples:

la mamma *mum*   **la camera** *room/bedroom*

However, a minority of words ending in -a are masculine:

il diploma *diploma*   **il profeta** *prophet*
il problema *problem*   **il pigiama** *pyjamas*

NOUNS ENDING IN -O

These are almost all **masculine** words, for example:

il bambino *child*   **il panino** *roll/sandwich*

However, some words ending in -o are feminine, including these:

la mano *hand*   **la moto** *motorbike (abbreviation of*
                            la motocicletta*)*
la radio   **l'auto** *car (abbreviation of* **l'automobile***)*

NOUNS ENDING IN -E

These words can be masculine or feminine. Eventually, after coming across them enough times, you will be able to tell their gender automatically. If in doubt, look them up in a dictionary.

il ristorante *restaurant (m.)*   **il nome** *name (m.)*
la televisione *television (f.)*   **la canzone** *song (f.)*

Some job titles ending in -e have a feminine equivalent ending in -a.

un infermiere *a male nurse*   **un'infermiera** *a female nurse*
un cameriere *a waiter*   **una cameriera** *a waitress*

OTHER NOUNS

Foreign nouns are mostly masculine, but some words borrowed from French are feminine (as in French):

il tram   **il film**   **la moquette** *carpet*
il gas   **lo sport**   **la brioche** *cake*

Words ending in -si are feminine:

l'oasi *oasis*   **l'analisi** *analysis/test*
la crisi *crisis/fit*   **la paralisi** *paralysis*

Words ending in -tà and -tù are also feminine:

la verità *truth*
la virtù *virtue*
la gioventù *youth*

Many first names have a 'mobile' gender. This gender shift is signalled by changing the ending: **Francesco/Francesca, Carlo/Carla.** Note that the first names **Andrea** and **Nicola** in Italian are boys' names only.

25a Mio marito, that's all you need!

Consider this:

Il mio marito si chiama Giovanni. ✗

This sentence is wrong because no definite article (**il**) is required in this particular use of the possessive adjective (**mio**). It should be like this:

Mio marito si chiama Giovanni. ✓

On the other hand, the sentence below has no article but is just as incorrect:

Miei bambini hanno due e quattro anni. ✗

The definite article (**i**) is needed before the plural form **miei**:

I miei bambini hanno due e quattro anni. ✓

Questi sono i miei genitori – mia madre e mio padre.

Let's explore the relationship between possessives and articles in a bit more detail.

First of all, possessive adjectives are usually placed before the noun they refer to, with which they always need to agree in gender and number. In the vast majority of cases (see page 66 for exceptions), they are preceded by a definite article, as in the examples listed in the table below.

	masculine singular	feminine singular	masculine plural	feminine plural
my	il mio cane	la mia casa	i miei soldi	le mie cose
your	il tuo cane	la tua casa	i tuoi soldi	le tue cose
his/her	il suo cane	la sua casa	i suoi soldi	le sue cose
our	il nostro cane	la nostra casa	i nostri soldi	le nostre cose
your	il vostro cane	la vostra casa	i vostri soldi	le vostre cose
their	il loro cane	la loro casa	i loro soldi	le loro cose

Note that the only adjective that doesn't change its ending is **loro**.

Sandra e Giacomo amano molto i loro cani.   *Sandra and Giacomo love their dogs very much.*

PROPRIO

Another useful adjective for talking about possession is **proprio**, meaning *my own, your own, their own,* etc. Like **loro**, **proprio** always needs the definite article before it.

il proprio onore   *one's own honour*

But be aware that **proprio** can have a completely different meaning:

È proprio vero.   *That's quite right.*
La posta è proprio lì a destra.   *The post office is right there, on the right.*

25b Mio marito, that's all you need!

Possessive adjectives are used alone, <u>without the article</u>, with words that refer to family members in the singular, such as:

madre	**mia madre**	*my mother*
padre	**mio padre**	*my father*
zio	**mio zio**	*my uncle*
zia	**mia zia**	*my aunt*
nipote	**mio nipote**	*my grandson/my nephew*
nipote	**mia nipote**	*my granddaughter/my niece*
cugino	**mio cugino**	*my cousin*
cugina	**mia cugina**	*my cousin*

The article, however, is to be kept in the following cases:

▶ When the possessive is **loro** or **proprio**:
   il loro zio   *their uncle*

▶ When referring to family members in the plural:
   le mie cugine   *my cousins (f.)*

▶ With the following colloquial nouns:
   il mio babbo   *my dad*
   la mia mamma   *my mum*

▶ With altered nouns, for example, where a diminutive suffix (**-ino/ina**) is added:
   la mia sorellina   *my little sister*

▶ When the noun is accompanied by a qualifying adjective or words that define it:
   mia zia   *my aunt*
   la mia cara zia   *my dear aunt*
   la mia zia di Vicenza   *my aunt from Vicenza*

Another common mistake is to include the possessive when it should be left out altogether. When ownership is self-evident, the possessive adjective is left out.

Ho perso il portafogli.	*I have lost my wallet.*
Non ho fatto i compiti.	*I haven't done my homework.*
Sta perdendo i capelli.	*He is losing his hair.*

Do not use possessives to talk about parts of the body (hair, head, hands, etc.) or things that clearly belong or relate to you, such as homework, umbrella, bed, driving licence or passport, to mention but a few. Should there be any confusion as to whose item it is, then the possessive can be added for extra clarity:

Ho perso l'ombrello.	*I've lost my umbrella.*
Ho perso l'ombrello di mia madre.	*I've lost my mother's umbrella.*
Ho perso il suo ombrello.	*I've lost her umbrella.*

Insight

Notice that *my house* typically translates as **casa mia**. That is, the possessive is idiomatically placed after the word **casa**:

Quante camere ci sono a casa tua?	*How many bedrooms are there in your house?*

The possessive can also be left out of the expression **casa mia** altogether:

Vado a casa il fine settimana.	*I'm going home at the weekend.*

26a Orders must be followed!

When learning Italian, you will have discovered that adjectives usually follow the noun they describe, as in these examples:

Gianluca ha comprato una macchina <u>usata</u>.   *Gianluca has bought a second-hand car.*

Mangio solamente piatti <u>vegetariani</u>.   *I only eat vegetarian dishes.*

But of course, if you stick too closely to that rule you will often be making a mistake.

Consider this sentence:

Ho fatto una passeggiata bella. ✗

It is not necessarily wrong, but sounds a bit odd and unnatural, because a native speaker would normally put **bella** <u>before</u> **passeggiata**:

Ho fatto una bella passeggiata. ✓   *I went for a nice walk.*

At the other end of the spectrum, there is no doubt that the sentence below is grammatically wrong:

Ecco il mio italiano amico. ✗

The correct version is:

Ecco il mio amico italiano. ✓   *Here's my Italian friend.*

Italiano is being used here as an adjective and should be placed after the noun **amico**.

Although adjectives generally follow nouns, as in **cielo** <u>blu</u> (*blue sky*) or **una giornata** <u>calda</u> (*a hot day*), some of the most common adjectives, listed below, are usually placed <u>before</u> the noun.

buono	**cattivo**	**bello**	**brutto**
giovane	**vecchio**	**grande**	**piccolo**
alto	**lungo**	**vero**	**bravo**
prossimo	**primo**	**ultimo**	**caro**

una bella giornata   *a fine/lovely day*
l'ultima lezione   *the last lesson*
la prossima partita   *the next match*

When placed before the noun, **bello** has four different masculine forms and follows the same rules as the definite article:

il bambino	**bel** bambino
i bambini	**bei** bambini
l'attore	**bell'**attore
gli attori	**begli** attori

Similarly, the forms of **buono** vary and correspond to the indefinite article:

un Natale *Christmas*	**Buon Natale** *Merry Christmas*
un anno *year*	**Buon Anno** *Happy New Year*
una domenica *Sunday*	**buona domenica** *have a good Sunday*
un'idea *idea*	**buon'idea** *good idea*

See Chapter 8 for situations where **buono, bello, grande** lose their final syllable.

However, even native speakers get this rule wrong sometimes, particularly if the word is plural and starts with a vowel or s + consonant. For instance, it wouldn't be uncommon to hear **belli attori** instead of **begli attori** or **belli studenti** instead of **begli studenti**.

26b Orders must be followed!

The normal position of an adjective is <u>after</u> the noun. This position tends to express neutral and objective or factual information (colour, physical state: **una maglia <u>rossa</u>, un piatto <u>caldo</u>**).

If placed <u>before</u> the noun, the adjective expresses participation and emotional involvement on the part of the speaker, therefore greater subjectivity.

There are several adjectives that can be placed before as well as after the noun, and depending on their position they acquire a slightly different meaning, or even a totally different one, so much so that in some cases their position becomes fixed to that meaning.

un <u>buon</u> amico = *a good friend*
un amico <u>buono</u> = *a friend who is good-natured and intrinsically a good person*

un <u>grande</u> uomo = *a great man, whose personality or achievements are remarkable*
un uomo <u>grande</u> = *a big or tall man*

un <u>alto</u> funzionario = *a high-level official*
un funzionario <u>alto</u> = *a tall official*

un <u>cattivo</u> consigliere = *a bad adviser*
un consigliere <u>cattivo</u> = *an adviser who is intrinsically a bad person*

una <u>cara</u> foto = *a much-loved/dear photograph*
una foto <u>cara</u> = *an expensive photograph*

una <u>bella</u> persona = *a good-natured person, with a nice personality*
una persona <u>bella</u> = *a good-looking person*

un <u>brutto</u> incidente = *a bad accident*
un uomo <u>brutto</u> = *an ugly-looking man*

una <u>brava</u> moglie = *a good wife*
una moglie <u>brava</u> a cucinare/stirare = *a wife good at cooking/ironing*

una <u>certa</u> cosa = *a certain thing, some vague undefined thing*
una cosa <u>certa</u> = *a sure thing, something that is certain*

When the adjective follows the noun, its meaning is literal. When the adjective is placed before the noun, the meaning is more figurative, abstract, poetic or emotional. This difference can be felt in this vivid example:

le scogliere <u>bianche</u> = *the white cliffs (in normal parlance)*
le <u>bianche</u> scogliere di Dover = *the white cliffs of Dover (holding a traditional, sentimental attachment for many British people)*

So if you want to describe something, for instance, a recent holiday, place **bello** and certain other adjectives <u>before</u> the nouns to add more life and participation to your account:

Ho passato una <u>stupenda</u> vacanza, ho visto molti <u>bei</u> monumenti e ho fatto molte <u>belle</u> foto.

Ho un ginocchio cattivo.

27 Italian is an agreeable language

Consider these examples:

1 **la bambino** ✗
2 **i gatto** ✗
3 **Lo studente leggi un libro.** ✗
4 **Ieri mangio troppo.** ✗

These phrases are unacceptable because they fail to follow various rules of agreement.

The first example contravenes the rule on <u>gender</u> agreement.
The correct form is:

1 **la bambina** ✓

or

   il bambino ✓

The second one goes against <u>number</u> agreement and should be:

2 **i gatti** ✓

or

   il gatto ✓

The third phrase doesn't follow the rule about <u>person</u> agreement (more on this in Chapter 29). It should be:

3 **Lo studente legge un libro.** ✓

The last one goes against <u>time</u> or <u>verb tense</u> agreement and should be:

4 **Ieri ho mangiato troppo.** ✓

Of course, in an English sentence words have to agree too and we automatically make alterations, for example, in plural nouns and in verbs: *I like football, my son <u>likes</u> football, my <u>sons</u> <u>like</u> football.* But there tend to be fewer changes than in Italian. It is useful to be aware of the different categories of rules on agreement, as set out above.

In order to make sure that all words in a sentence agree, it is useful to identify the central word that all the others depend upon and should agree with. For instance, in **la mia cara sorella,** the central word is **sorella,** and the other words – definite article (**la**) and adjectives (**mia cara**) – must have a form that matches it.

The table below gives some more examples of typical incorrect phrases where the agreement has been overlooked or done wrongly (✗), together with its correct format (✓).

✗	✓	
esercizi difficile	esercizi difficili	*difficult exercises*
paesi esotico	paesi esotici	*exotic countries*
qualche volte	qualche volta	*sometimes/at times*
l'edicole	le edicole	*newspaper kiosks*
una buono vacanza	una buona vacanza	*a good holiday*
sei mese	sei mesi	*six months*
molte insegnante	molte insegnanti	*many (female) teachers*
molti elefante	molti elefanti	*many elephants*
non ho le chiave	non ho le chiavi	*I don't have the keys*
fagiolini verde	fagiolini verdi	*green beans*
ogni giorni	ogni giorno	*every day*

28 Many, few and near: do they agree?

As we have seen, agreement in gender and number is an important requirement in Italian and is fertile ground for mistakes. The words **molto**, **poco** and **vicino**, in particular, seem to be affected by a chronic lack of agreement.

Look at these sentences:

Hanno molto problemi. ✕
Abbiamo poco carne in frigo. ✕
La città più vicino è a quattro chilometri di distanza. ✕

And here are the correct forms:

Hanno molt<u>i</u> problemi.✓	*They've got a lot of problems.*
Abbiamo poc<u>a</u> carne in frigo. ✓	*We haven't got much meat in the fridge.*
La città più vicin<u>a</u> è a quattro chilometri di distanza. ✓	*The nearest town is 4 km away.*

However, **molto**, **poco** and **vicino** don't always need to agree; it all depends whether they are being used as adjectives or adverbs. This is where some of the confusion tends to arise.

When they play the role of <u>adjectives</u>, they qualify a noun and therefore need to agree with it; when their role is as <u>adverbs</u>, they modify a verb, an adjective or another adverb, and no agreement is necessary.

'MOLTO'

Martina ha molti soldi.   *Martina has lots of money.*

– here **molto** is an adjective, qualifying **soldi**, and therefore it has to agree with **soldi**.

Marco mi ama molto.   *Marco loves me a lot.*

– here **molto** is an adverb, qualifying the verb **ama**, so there is no need for agreement.

Here is another example of **molto** used as an adjective, agreeing with the noun, and then as an adverb without agreement:

Oggi non ho <u>molto tempo</u> per parlare.	*Today I don't have much time to talk.*
Hanno speso <u>molto</u> per il matrimonio.	*They spent a lot on their wedding.*

'POCO'

Abbiamo solo pochi minuti.   *We only have a few minutes.*

– here **pochi** is an adjective and has to agree with **minuti**.

Lo spettacolo comincia tra poco.   *The show will start soon.*

– here **poco** is an adverb qualifying **comincia** – no need for agreement.

Again, the next two examples use **poco** as an adjective and as an adverb:

<u>**Poche cose**</u> **mi fanno ridere oggi.**	*Few things make me laugh nowadays.*
Silvia è una persona che si accontenta di <u>poco</u>.	*Silvia is contented with little./It doesn't take much to make Silvia happy.*

'VICINO'

Vicino acts in a similar way. For instance, the question **Quanto dista la stazione?** (*How far is the station?*) could have two different answers:

1 **È vicina.** *It's near.*
2 **È vicino.** *It's near.*

In the first answer, **vicina** agrees in gender and number with the feminine word **stazione**, because it plays the role of adjective and qualifies **stazione**.

In the second answer no agreement is necessary because **vicino** refers to the notion of 'vicinity/proximity'. It doesn't qualify the word **stazione**: it is used as an adverb, not an adjective, and therefore doesn't need to agree with anything.

29a Verbal agreements

As with nouns and adjectives, the relationship between subjects and verbs is also characterized by agreement: the subject and the verb must reflect the same grammatical information in terms of person, number and, in some cases, gender.

Below you will find some mistakes relating to person agreement:

Mio fratello faccio il cuoco. ✗
Io va al pub il venerdì. ✗

The correct forms are:

Mio fratello fa il cuoco. ✓   *My brother is a cook.*
Io vado al pub il venerdì. ✓   *I go to the pub on Fridays.*

Of course, the subject pronoun **io** is usually omitted in Italian: see Chapter 17. So, that last example should really be:

Vado al pub il venerdì.

The pronoun was included there simply to stress the point about agreement.

Here are two examples of number agreement, focusing on singular and plural.

La donna cantavano. ✗
La donna cantava. ✓   *The woman was singing.*

Le donne cantava. ✗
Le donne cantavano. ✓   *The women were singing.*

If you can't always remember which verb endings to use for
I, you, he/she, etc., check the verb tables in a dictionary or
your textbook, until you know them automatically.

Hint: in the present and imperfect tenses, for the vast
majority of verbs, the difference between the first and second
person singular (the forms for *I* and *you*) is always the same:
-o for the first person, -i for the second.

Present:

(io)	canto	parto	scrivo
(tu)	canti	parti	scrivi

Imperfect:

(io)	cantavo	partivo	ero	avevo
(tu)	cantavi	partivi	eri	avevi

29b Verbal agreements

As we saw in 29a, a verb must agree in person and number with its subject.

Let's now have a look at gender agreement, which affects the perfect tense (**passato prossimo**) when it is formed with **essere**. (See Chapter 30 for more on the perfect tense and in particular, which verbs use **essere** and which use **avere** to form the perfect tense.)

Consider these mistakes:

1 Ieri Marta è andat<u>o</u> al cinema. ✗
2 Lorena e Franca, quando siete partit<u>o</u>? ✗

In both cases the subject is feminine: **Marta, Lorena e Franca.** With **essere**, the verb (the past participle) needs to agree with the subject, as follows:

Ieri Marta è andat<u>a</u> al cinema. ✓	*Yesterday Marta went to the cinema.*
Lorena e Franca, quando siete partit<u>e</u>? ✓	*Lorena and Franca, when did you leave?*

In the table below you will find all the possible agreement combinations that occur in the perfect tense when conjugating **partire** (*to leave*).

	masculine	*feminine*
singular	**sono partito**	**sono partita**
	sei partito	**sei partita**
	è partito	**è partita**
plural	**siamo partiti**	**siamo partite**
	siete partiti	**siete partite**
	sono partiti	**sono partite**

The paragraph below contains four perfect tense verbs, underlined.

Quando avevo 14 anni <u>sono andata</u> in gita con la scuola. <u>Siamo andati</u> a Pompei e Sorrento. <u>Mi sono divertita</u> molto con i miei amici. <u>Abbiamo riso</u> molto.

When I was 14 years old, I went on a school trip. We went to Pompeii and Sorrento. I enjoyed myself a lot with my friends. We laughed a lot.

Look again at those four perfect tense verbs.

▶ In the infinitive, they are **andare** (*to go*), **andare, divertirsi** (*to enjoy oneself*), **ridere** (*to laugh*).

▶ The first three verbs form the perfect tense with **essere** and the past participle must agree with the subject: **(io) sono andata, (noi) siamo andati, (io) mi sono divertita.** You can tell that the speaker is female and that both male and female students went on the school trip.

▶ The fourth forms the perfect tense with **avere**; the past participle **riso** does not need any agreement.

'Siamo andati a Pompei'

30a Essere o avere? That is the question

A very frequent mistake occurs when the wrong auxiliary verb (**essere** or **avere**) is used to form the perfect tense (**passato prossimo**):

Ho andato al pub. ✗
Sono fatto una passeggiata. ✗

The correct form of these verbs is:

<u>**Sono andato**</u> **al pub.**   *I went to the pub.* ✓
<u>**Ho fatto**</u> **una passeggiata.**   *I went for a walk.* ✓

USE 'ESSERE' IN THE FOLLOWING CASES:

▶ with all reflexive verbs:
Mi sono lavato le mani.   *I washed my hands.*

▶ with verbs of movement (going from one place to another). These verbs include: **andare, arrivare, entrare, cadere, tornare, uscire, venire, partire, restare, ritornare.**
Siamo andati a casa.   *We went home.*

▶ with verbs expressing a physical change. These verbs include: **essere, nascere, morire, diventare, ingrassare, dimagrire:**
È ingrassato.   *He has put on weight.*

▶ with the passive form:
La mia casa è stata costruita nel 1980.   *My house was built in 1980.*

▶ with impersonal verbs:
È stato necessario chiamare la polizia.   *It was necessary to call the police.*

USE 'AVERE' IN THE FOLLOWING CASES:

▶ with a large number of verbs used in everyday phrases, such as **comprare, fare, guardare, mangiare, studiare, scrivere, leggere, dormire, dire**.

I ragazzi hanno fatto i compiti.	*The boys have done their homework.*
Hai scritto quella lettera?	*Have you written that letter?*

Even with these **avere** verbs it's not always clear-cut: when they are transformed into reflexive verbs, which occurs particularly in spoken Italian, they have to take **essere**. See Chapter 33 (Insight) for more on this.

Mi sono comprata una bella borsa.	*I bought myself a lovely handbag.*

▶ with **dovere/volere/potere**, when these verbs stand alone:
Non ho potuto. *I wasn't able to/I couldn't.*

▶ with **dovere/potere/volere**, when they are preceded by a pronoun:
Gli hanno dovuto dire la verità. *They had to tell him the truth.*

Insight

For **dovere, potere, volere**, when used with another verb, go with **essere** or **avere** depending on which one the other verb would normally take. For example, **partire** normally takes **essere**, while **mangiare** normally takes **avere**. The following examples show **dovere** used (correctly) with both **essere** and **avere**:

Sono partito il giorno dopo.	*I left the day after.*
<u>**Sono dovuto**</u> **partire il giorno dopo.**	*I had to leave the day after.*

Hanno mangiato al ristorante.	*They ate at the restaurant.*
<u>**Hanno dovuto**</u> **mangiare al ristorante.**	*They had to eat at the restaurant.*

Just bear in mind that occasionally, particularly in spoken Italian, native speakers get this rule wrong too!

30b Essere o avere? That is the question

It is important to be aware that many verbs are somewhat 'promiscuous' and will be accompanied by either **essere** or **avere** in compound tenses, depending on the message we want to convey. For these verbs, as a general rule, the auxiliary verb **essere** will appear when the verbs are used as intransitives, whereas the auxiliary **avere** will be found when they are used as transitives.

Whenever I mention the word <u>transitive</u> the typical student usually wants to run for cover! But it doesn't have to be a scary subject; it's actually quite straightforward. Let me explain the difference between transitive and intransitive verbs.

TRANSITIVE VERBS

Transitive verbs have or are able to have a direct or indirect object. In the sentence **Giorgio mangia una mela** (*Giorgio is eating an apple*) the direct object is **la mela**.

In some cases the object is implicit and not actually named, as in the sentence below:

Carla sta mangiando.   *Carla is eating.*

Carla is eating something but we don't know what the object is left out and implicit. However, **mangiare** remains a transitive verb.

Here are two more examples of transitive verbs in sentences, this time in the perfect tense:

<u>Ho fatto</u> molte fotografie.   *I took lots of pictures.*
<u>Abbiamo bevuto</u> un cappuccino.   *We drank a cappuccino.*

Some verbs such as **telefonare** and **dare** may have an object that requires the help of a 'crutch' in the form of a preposition.

In the following sentence: **Telefono a Maria,** the word **Maria** is used as an indirect object, that is, the indirect receiver of the action. You can tell that it's indirect as it has the preposition **a** before it. In this example: **Ho dato il mio libro a Maria,** the verb has both a direct object (**il mio libro**) and an indirect object (**Maria**).

INTRANSITIVE VERBS

Intransitive verbs are those that do not act on an object. These are verbs such as **correre, dormire, nascere, partire, andare.**

These sentences all contain intransitive verbs. The verbs are in the perfect tense, some using **avere** and some using **essere:**

Hanno dormito più di dieci ore.	*They slept for over ten hours.*
Fabrizio è andato in vacanza in Toscana.	*Fabrizio went on holiday in Tuscany.*
Sono ritornata dopo una settimana.	*I came back after a week.*
Il tempo è stato bello.	*The weather was good.*

Several verbs can be both transitive and intransitive, for instance **finire, cambiare, diminuire, aumentare, continuare, migliorare, peggiorare.** In their transitive form the action is directed to an object. In their intransitive form, the action is directed back to the subject.

Ho cambiato i soldi.   *I changed the money.*

– there is a clear subject and a clear direct object (transitive form).

La vita è cambiata.   *Life has changed.*

– the subject 'receives' the action and there is no other object (intransitive form).

If in doubt whether a verb is transitive or intransitive (or both!), looking the verb up in a good dictionary or verb book should help.

31a Perfect vs imperfect

Ieri andavamo al ristorante. ✗

The sentence above is wrong because the speaker uses the imperfect **andavamo** to talk about an event that happened yesterday and is now over and done with: *we went to the restaurant*. The perfect tense (**passato prossimo**) should have been used instead:

Ieri <u>siamo andati</u> al ristorante. ✓ *Yesterday we went to the restaurant.*

or of course, if the group who went to the restaurant were all female, then use the feminine ending for **andati**:

Ieri <u>siamo andate</u> al ristorante. ✓ *Yesterday we went to the restaurant.*

The imperfect isn't right because it is used for other purposes such as:

▶ to express habitual or repeated actions in the past, in other words, to say what used to happen or what we used to do/ would do in the past,
▶ to describe people, places, physical or mental states in the past,
▶ to set out the background of an event.

The sentences below give examples of those purposes.

▶ habitual action:
Da bambina <u>andavo</u> al mare ogni estate.
As a child I would go to the seaside every summer

▶ description:
Mia nonna <u>era</u> molto gentile.
My grandmother was very kind.
Negli anni 50 l'Internet non <u>esisteva</u>.
In the 1950s the internet didn't exist.
<u>Ero</u> molto felice di vivere lì.
I was very happy to live there.

▶ background or interrupted event:

Ieri <u>andavamo</u> al ristorante *Yesterday we <u>were going</u>*
quando improvvisamente *to the restaurant when*
<u>ha cominciato a nevicare</u>. *suddenly <u>it started snowing</u>.*

– **andavamo** is the background to the event **ha cominciato a nevicare**, which is expressed with a perfect tense.

By contrast, the perfect tense (**passato prossimo**), formed with **avere** or **essere** + past participle of the main verb, is used to express an action or event that has a beginning and an end. The time or duration of the action can be stated in the sentence or can be implicit.

<u>Ho portato</u> fuori il cane. *I've taken the dog out.*

– the time frame is not stated.

Ieri sera Marta e Carolina *Last night Marta and Carolina*
<u>sono andate</u> al cinema. *went to the cinema.*

– the time frame is expressed by **ieri sera**.

Read this brief account of a holiday, to sense the combination of perfect and imperfect tense verbs.

L'ultima volta che <u>sono andata</u> in Italia, il tempo <u>era</u> bello e <u>faceva</u> caldo. C'<u>erano</u> 29 gradi. Prima di ripartire <u>ho comprato</u> una bella borsa di pelle. Il viaggio di ritorno in aereo <u>è durato</u> tre ore.

The last time I went to Italy, the weather was nice and it was hot. It was 29 degrees. Before leaving I bought a beautiful leather bag. The return journey by plane lasted three hours.

Sono andata requires the perfect tense, because the action expressed had a clear beginning and end, as did the buying of a leather bag (**ho comprato**) and the duration of the flight (**è durato**). Three other verbs (**era, faceva, erano**) are in the imperfect tense because they describe what the weather was like, without specific beginning and end points.

31b Perfect vs imperfect

Note the different meanings of **sapere** and **conoscere**, depending on whether they are conjugated in the perfect or imperfect.

'SAPERE'

Ieri <u>ho saputo</u> che Serena si è sposata!

Yesterday I found out that Serena got married!

– perfect tense, expressing a single, one-off event that occurred during a specified time frame; the time of the event may be explicit or may be left out.

<u>Non sapevo</u> che lo scoiattolo rosso è in pericolo di estinzione.

I didn't know that the red squirrel is in danger of extinction.

– imperfect tense, describing the state of our knowledge at some point in the past, before we found out something new.

'CONOSCERE'

<u>Ci siamo conosciuti</u> nel 1980.

We met in 1980.

– perfect tense, expressing a specific event that happened once.

Quando ci siamo trasferiti nella nuova città non <u>conoscevamo</u> nessuno.

When we moved to the new town we didn't know anybody.

– imperfect tense, describing an ongoing state of affairs; you can't say when the state of 'not knowing anybody' started or when it finished.

As illustrated above, you can use **conoscere** as an alternative to **incontrare** to say that you met somebody for the first time:

Ho conosciuto mio marito a Roma.   *I met my husband in Rome.*
Ho incontrato mio marito a Roma.   *I met my husband in Rome.*

As you can see, the imperfect, by definition, is 'not perfect', it lacks definition; it doesn't tell you when something started and when it ended.

Insight

Be careful when translating a phrase that contains 'would' in English, as it may need to be translated as an imperfect or a conditional, depending on the context.

When I was a child I would play every day with my best friend.
Imperfect:
Da piccolo giocavo tutti i giorni con la mia migliore amica.

I would play with you but it's late and I have to go home.
Conditional:
Giocherei con te ma è tardi e devo tornare a casa.

L'abbiamo saputo troppo tardi.

We found out too late.

32a Live in the present, look to the future

Consider this sentence, which has **andare** in the future tense:

Stasera andrò a casa di Alessio. ✗

This kind of error is all to do with style and register, as in Italian the future tense is not used very often in conversation. The sentence above uses the future when it would be much more common to use the present; it's a bit like wearing your best shoes at home instead of wearing your slippers!

From a grammar point of view, it is totally acceptable to use the future to describe a future event, but it is not what Italians would normally do in everyday conversation. If you use the future tense, your way of talking and expressing yourself sounds formal, and there is no need for that in normal conversation. It's like saying *I shall go* in English. Going back to the previous example, what you would hear instead is:

Stasera vado a casa di Alessio. ✓   *Tonight I'm going to Alessio's house.*

Of course if you intend to impress your audience or sound more formal, or need to give a presentation, do use the future instead.

The ideal setting for the future tense is formal speech. You will hear it, and have opportunities to use it, in the specific contexts and circumstances listed below.

THE WEATHER FORECAST

Ci saranno piovaschi sul versante adriatico.
There will be scattered showers on the Adriatic coast.

PREDICTIONS AND HOROSCOPES

Le carte dicono che incontrerai presto l'uomo della tua vita.
The cards say you will soon meet the man of your life.

**Venere e Mercurio ti aiuteranno a mantenere il buonumore.
Una nuova amicizia si rafforzerà.**
*Venus and Mercury will help you stay in a good mood. A new
friendship will get stronger.*

PROMISES, PLEDGES AND THREATS

Chiarirò tutto, te lo prometto.
I'll clarify everything, I promise.

Ti amerò per sempre.
I will love you forever.

Te ne pentirai!
You'll regret it!

Ti porterò sulla Luna!

E l'anello di diamanti?

LONG-TERM PLANS AND PROJECTS

Il progetto CityLife farà di Milano una metropoli europea.
The CityLife project will turn Milan into a European metropolis.

Quando sarò grande farò l'attore.
When I grow up I'll be an actor.

TO EXPRESS A STRONG PROBABILITY OR AN OPINION ON THE LIKELIHOOD OF SOMETHING

Se continua a fumare così si ammalerà.
If he carries on smoking like that he will get ill.

Sarà stato Alberto a bussare alla porta.
It must have been Alberto who knocked at the door.

IN A FIXED EXPRESSION SUCH AS 'TI DIRÒ'

Ti dirò, mi piacerebbe andare a vivere in Africa.
I tell you, I'd like to go and live in Africa.

32b Live in the present, look to the future

The first two pages of Chapter 32 explained that if you use the future tense in normal conversation, it will give you an aura of formality that is often unnecessary and unnatural.

Therefore, whenever you want to say what you will be doing in the immediate future or even longer term, or to make a polite request, all you need is the <u>present</u> tense:

Sandro <u>esce</u> stasera.	*Sandro is going out tonight.*
Domani <u>vado</u> in banca.	*Tomorrow I'm going to the bank.*
Tra due anni <u>mi iscrivo</u> all'università.	*In two years' time I'll enrol at university.*
Ti <u>aiuto</u> a portare la valigia?	*Shall I help you carry the case?*

When you want to translate English phrases about the future based on 'going to do something', such as *She's going to visit Italy next year* or *I'm going to do my homework later*, make sure you avoid beginning with the equivalent of *to go* – **andare**. Head straight for the present tense.

L'anno prossimo visita l'Italia.	*She's going to visit Italy next year*
Faccio i compiti più tardi.	*I'm going to do my homework later.*
A che ora ci incontriamo?	*What time are we going to meet?*

THE PRESENT CONTINUOUS

I'm going to the bank tomorrow translates as **Vado in banca domani,** but if you want to emphasize that something is happening at this very moment (i.e. *I'm just writing an email right now*), use the present continuous rather than the present tense.

The present continuous is made up of the verb **stare,** followed by the main verb ending in -**ando** or -**endo** (this form is called the gerund – see page 135).

| Che stai facendo adesso? | *What are you doing right now?* |
| Sto scrivendo. | *I'm writing.* |

But don't be tempted to overuse this form, as Italian, unlike English, uses the normal present tense much more often than the present continuous.

Insight

Prima di finire questo capitolo ...   *Before finishing this chapter ...*

The English structure *before doing something* is expressed in Italian by **prima di** and an infinitive. Don't be tempted to use a verb form ending **-ando** or **-endo** for this.

| **Prima di andare a lavorare faccio colazione.** | *Before going to work I have breakfast.* |
| **Prima di uscire di casa chiudi la finestra.** | *Before going out of the house close the window.* |

'Prima di finire questo capitolo ...'

33 Reflect on reflexives

In Italian there are many reflexive verbs. A verb is defined as reflexive when subject and object coincide, as in **mi alzo**, *I get up*. When a verb is reflexive, the action turns back or 'reflects' on the subject. Such verbs must always be preceded by a reflexive pronoun (**mi**, in the example **mi alzo**), which is what distinguishes them from ordinary verbs.

The most common reflexive verbs are: **lavarsi** (*to get washed*), **alzarsi** (*to get up*), **svegliarsi** (*to wake up*), **vestirsi** (*to get dressed*), **sedersi** (*to sit down*), **preoccuparsi** (*to be worried*).

Here are examples of **lavarsi**, a typical reflexive verb:

Davide si lava.   *Davide is getting washed/having a wash.*
Francesca si lava i capelli.   *Francesca is washing her hair.*

Note that reflexive verbs can have an ordinary counterpart which doesn't require a reflexive pronoun:

Francesca lava la macchina.   *Francesca is washing the car.*

Having said that, one of the most common mistakes students make with reflexive verbs is to forget to include the reflexive pronoun when it is in fact required. For instance, they write:

1 **Io alzo alle sette.** ✗
2 **Siamo divertiti molto.** ✗
3 **Gabriele e Giuliana incontrano tutti i giorni.** ✗

These sentences are all missing the reflexive pronoun. The correct forms are:

1 **Io <u>mi alzo</u> alle sette.** ✓   *I get up at seven.*
2 **<u>Ci siamo</u> divertiti molto.** ✓   *We enjoyed ourselves very much.*
3 **Gabriele e Giuliana <u>si incontrano</u> tutti i giorni.** ✓   *Gabriele and Giuliana meet every day.*

Reflexive verbs can also be used to express reciprocal or mutual actions (as in the case of example 3 above), when meaning 'one another' or 'each other':

Le tre sorelle si aiutano. *The three sisters help one another.*
Paolo e Carla si sposano domani. *Paolo and Carla are getting married tomorrow.*

Insight

mi lavo = lavo me stesso = *I wash myself*

This is clearly a reflexive verb. On the other hand, consider a sentence like **Mi sono mangiato un bel gelato,** *I ate a nice ice-cream.* The pronoun **mi** is placed before **mangiare**, although this verb normally is not reflexive: **ho mangiato**.

A sentence like this is usually found in colloquial Italian, where **mi** (or any other reflexive pronoun) functions as a reinforcement, highlighting the personal involvement in the action. In this example it serves to emphasize the satisfaction or pleasure felt by the speaker in eating the ice-cream.

34a Piacere: put it back to front

Consider these three sentences:

1 **Nel tempo libero mi piaccio fare spese.** ✗
2 **Quel film non mi ha piaciuto.** ✗
3 **I miei genitori non piace la spiaggia.** ✗

In the first sentence, the mistake lies within the word **piaccio**.
What we need instead is:

Nel tempo libero <u>mi piace</u> fare   *In my free time I like going*
spese. ✓   *shopping.*

In the second sentence, what is wrong is the auxiliary verb **ha**.
The perfect tense (**passato prossimo**) of **piacere** is formed with
essere, not **avere**:

Quel film non mi <u>è</u> piaciuto. ✓   *I didn't like that film.*

In the third example, the preposition **a** is missing at the very
beginning (it combines with **i** to form **ai**):

<u>Ai</u> miei genitori non piace la   *My parents don't like the beach.*
spiaggia. ✓

Piacere is a verb that is very often misused and misunderstood.
It means *to please*, so you can instantly see that there is no direct
equivalence with the verb *to like*. The confusion arises because
in Italian what you like is the subject of your sentence, whereas
in English it is the other way round and the person who likes
something is the subject.

As a consequence, in Italian you will only need two present tense
forms of this verb to say what you like and dislike: **piace** and
piacciono (*it pleases* and *they please*). The statement: *I like red
wine*, in Italian translates as: *Red wine pleases me*.

Note that the pronoun, the word for *me* – **mi** in Italian – goes before the verb:

Mi piace il vino.   *I like red wine./Red wine pleases me.*

If what you like is singular, or is expressed by a verb in the infinitive form, **piace** must be used (even if there is a plural noun after the verb, as in sentence no. 3):

1 **Mi piace questo cinema.**   *I like this cinema.*
2 **Mi piace nuotare e giocare**   *I like swimming and playing*
   a tennis.   *tennis.*
3 **Non mi piace mangiare**   *I don't like eating too many*
   troppi dolci.   *sweet things.*

If what you like is a plural noun, **piacciono** must be used:

Mi piacciono questi fiori.   *I like these flowers.*

34b Piacere: put it back to front

In the first two pages of Chapter 34 we saw that whereas in English <u>we</u> are pleased, in Italian it's the other way round: <u>something</u> pleases us:

Mi piace la musica moderna.   *I like modern music.*

Once you've got used to this, it's not difficult.

But there's one thing you need to remember. If the person being pleased isn't represented by a pronoun (*I, you, he, she,* etc. in English) you need to add the preposition **a**, combined with the definite article if necessary:

Anna likes modern music. = To Anna modern music is pleasing.
<u>A</u> Anna piace la musica moderna.

Giorgio likes football. = To Giorgio football is pleasing.
<u>A</u> Giorgio piace il calcio.

My children don't like vegetables. = Vegetables are not pleasing
to (the) my children.
<u>Ai</u> miei figli non piacciono le verdure.

Another way to use **piacere** is to add a stressed or emphatic pronoun after the preposition **a**. This is used for stronger emphasis, to establish a contrast or correct a mistake:

<u>A lui</u> piace molto il cricket ma   *He likes cricket very much but*
   <u>a me</u> non piace per niente.   *I don't like it at all.*

Ho detto che è <u>a lui</u> che piace   *I said that it is he who likes*
   cucinare, non <u>a lei</u>.   *cooking, not she.*

The table below lists all the pronouns you can use with the verb **piacere**. Remember to change **piace** to **piacciono** when the thing that you like (or dislike) is plural.

	unstressed	stressed
I like	**mi piace**	**a me piace**
you like	**ti piace**	**a te piace**
he likes	**gli piace**	**a lui piace**
she likes	**le piace**	**a lei piace**
you like (formal)	**le piace**	**a lei piace**
we like	**ci piace**	**a noi piace**
you like (plural)	**vi piace**	**a voi piace**
they like	**gli piace**	**a loro piace**

Insight

It is wrong to say **mi dispiace** if what you mean is *I don't like it*. Use **mi dispiace** to say that you are sorry. Use **non mi piace** to say that you don't like something.

This chapter has focused mostly on **piacere** in the present tense. One sentence in the middle of page 94 contains an example of **piacere** in the perfect tense: **mi è piaciuto**.

You may want to use **piacere** in other tenses and forms, as in the following examples.

Mi è piaciuta molto la fontana di Trevi a Roma.
I very much liked the Trevi Foutain in Rome. (perfect tense)

Mi piacerebbe andare ad Alberobello.
I would like to go to Alberobello. (conditional)

Mi sarebbe piaciuto visitare Ercolano.
I would have liked to visit Ercolano. (past conditional)

Choosing the right words

See Chapter 38

35 Careful with what you enjoy!

Consider this sentence:

Quando sono andato in Italia ho goduto la cucina italiana e il vino. ✗

What the speaker had in mind to say was: *When I went to Italy I enjoyed Italian cooking and wine.* His sentence attempts to translate the verb *enjoy* with its dictionary equivalent: **godere**. In the vast majority of cases, this is inappropriate, as **godere** and *enjoy* are not perfect substitutes for each other.

The verb **godere** has a more limited use in Italian and it is much more emotionally charged; so much so that it can take on sexual undertones. Therefore if you enjoy a meal, the use of **godere** would not be very appropriate, however divine the experience might be! Generally you should not use **godere** to say how much you appreciate something; instead, find a different way of expressing it, as in the examples below.

Non hanno gradito il suo senso dell'umorismo.	*They didn't enjoy his sense of humour.*
Le è piaciuto molto lo spettacolo.	*She enjoyed the show a lot.*
Mi ha fatto molto piacere vederti.	*I really enjoyed seeing you.*
Al cane è piaciuta molto la passeggiata nel bosco.	*The dog enjoyed the walk in the woods.*
Divertiti alla festa!	*Enjoy the party!*
Fai buone vacanze!	*Enjoy the holiday!*

Godere should be used with caution as it expresses a particularly intense enjoyment, similar to the English words *rejoice* or *revel*:

Godo della vostra felicità.	*I rejoice in seeing you happy.*
Godiamo della nostra nuova libertà.	*We revel in our new freedom.*

It is also mainly found in certain styles and registers, for instance in written descriptions, formal speech or proverbs, as well as in pronominal forms of the verb (where it is accompanied by one or two pronouns) such as **godersi** or **godersela**. Note that the pronominal form is used equally in written and spoken Italian.

Se la gode nel prenderlo in giro.	*He/She really enjoys making fun of him.*
Goditela finchè sei giovane.	*Enjoy it/Have fun while you are young.*

More formal uses of **godere** are:

godere dei diritti essenziali	*to enjoy basic rights*
Anna gode di ottima salute.	*Anna enjoys very good health.*
La casa gode di un'ottima vista sul mare.	*The house enjoys a very good view of the sea.*
Un film divertente da godere in alta definizione	*A funny film to enjoy in high definition*
Gode di fama mondiale.	*He enjoys worldwide fame.*

... and finally, a proverb:

Chi si accontenta gode.	*Those who are contented with what they've got, will rejoice in it.*

Another verb similar to *to enjoy* is *to have a good time*, which must <u>not</u> be translated word-for-word from English; if you do, you may be misunderstood as asking about the weather – **il tempo!** It is necessary to find another turn of phrase that expresses the same concept:

Marta si è divertita molto alla festa.	*Marta had a really good time at the party.*
Franco è stato bene con gli amici.	*Franco had a good time with his friends.*

36 Prendere: don't take it for granted

Prendere is another unfortunate casualty of mistranslation. The vast majority of students make the mistake of translating it literally, as in this typical example:

Prendo il pranzo. ✗

Here is the correct version:

Pranzo. ✓   *I take/have lunch. (from the verb **pranzare**)*

You can only say **prendo il pranzo** if what you mean is *I pick lunch up* or *I collect lunch*:

Prendo il pranzo dalla cucina e lo porto in sala da pranzo.	*I pick lunch up from the kitchen and take it to the dining room.*

Here are some more examples where *take* cannot be translated as prendere:

<u>Ceno</u> alle otto di sera.	*I take/have dinner at 8 pm.*
<u>Faccio</u> colazione.	*I take/have breakfast.*
Giorgio <u>fa</u> una passeggiata prima di cena.	*Giorgio takes a walk before dinner.*
Devi <u>fare</u> più esercizio fisico.	*You need to take more exercise.*
Gianna <u>fa</u> una doccia.	*Gianna is taking a shower.*
<u>Portiamo</u> fuori il bambino a fare una passeggiata.	*We're taking the baby out for a walk.*
<u>Porto</u> una bottiglia di vino alla cena di Marilena.	*I'll take a bottle of wine to Marilena's dinner.*
Ti <u>porto</u> all'aeroporto.	*I'll take you to the airport.*
<u>Vado</u> in vacanza ogni anno.	*I take a holiday every year.*
Il dottore mi ha detto di <u>fare</u> un'analisi del sangue.	*The doctor told me to take a blood test.*

As you can see, *take* can be translated in many different ways, while its literal translation tends to be reserved to the act of picking up or collecting something or somebody. If the meaning is *to go and collect somebody or something*, it often has **andare** (or **venire**) in front:

Vado a prendere mia figlia alle 3.30.	*I am picking up my daughter at 3.30.*
Vanno a prendere Maria all'aeroporto.	*They are going to collect Maria from the airport.*
Ho lasciato la cena in cucina, vai a prenderla.	*I left dinner in the kitchen, go and get it.*
Aspetta lì, vengo a prenderti.	*Wait there, I'll come and collect you.*

In all circumstances where you are buying something or having something to drink or eat, **prendere** is what you need:

Per primo prendo spaghetti alle vongole.	*For the main course I'll have spaghetti with clams.*
Prendo la borsa di pelle nera.	*I'll have/buy the black leather bag.*
Prendiamo una birra al bar?	*Shall we have a beer at the bar?*

37 Going shopping at night

It's all too easy for learners of any language to translate literally
from their own language. If you are tempted to do this, though,
you will at best produce some very odd-sounding Italian, and at
worst confuse your listener completely! This chapter focuses on
two common mistakes which English speakers make.

EVENING AND NIGHT

I've noticed time and time again that some confusion surrounds
the words **sera** and **notte**. In Italian the word **sera** is much more
widespread than **notte**, because the latter only refers to the later
hours, say from 11 pm or midnight, until the early hours of the
morning. If you mean *evening* rather than *night*, say **sera**:

Domani notte vado a teatro. ✗
Domani sera vado a teatro. ✓   *Tomorrow night I'm going to the*
    theatre.

Hence, *goodnight* is usually **buonasera**, unless it's very late at night
or you are about to go to bed:

Vado a letto, buonanotte. ✓   *I'm going to bed. Goodnight.*

HOW MUCH IS IT?

Consider this dialogue:

– Quanto costa?   *– How much is it?*
– È 30 euro. ✗
– 30 euro. ✓   *– It's 30 €.*

When saying how much something costs, do not start with **È**, even
though the results may sound rather blunt to the English ear. Leave
out the verb altogether and simply state the price; don't make the
mistake of translating word for word from English to Italian.

– Quanto costa la camicia?   *How much is the shirt?*
– 30 euro.

In a market or shop, you might come across other verbs used to state the price of an item: **venire** and **fare**. You can use **venire** to ask the price of a single item or the total sale price (as you would in English: *how much does it* <u>come</u> *to?*). Use **fare** when asking the price of fruit and vegetables or other items that are sold by their weight:

– Quanto <u>vengono</u> le mele al chilo?   *How much are the apples?*
– Le mele <u>vengono</u> due euro al chilo.   *The apples are 2€ a kilo.*
– Quanto <u>viene</u>?   *How much does it come to?*

– Quanto <u>fanno</u> le patate al chilo?   *How much are the potatoes per kilo?*
– Le patate <u>fanno</u> un euro al chilo.   *The potatoes are 1€ per kilo.*

To recap, avoid the first of these models:

Le patate sono un euro al chilo. ✗
Le patate costano/fanno/vengono un euro al chilo. ✓

Insight

You might hear a shop assistant telling you how much you have to pay in total for your shopping, starting the sentence with **sono**, like this:

Sono 50 euro.

But **sono** + total amount to pay is what the shop assistant would say, not you, the customer.

38 Don't fail to say how to succeed!

'SUCCEDERE' DOESN'T MEAN SUCCEED

The Italian verb **succedere** means *to happen*, or *to occur*, but never *to succeed*:

Potrebbe succedere un incidente.	*An accident could happen.*
Che succede? Perché gridate?	*What is happening? Why are you screaming?*
Cosa ti è successo? Perché piangi?	*What has happened to you (what's the matter)? Why are you crying?*

There are various ways you can translate *to succeed* in Italian; one of them is to use **avere successo**:

Perché Facebook ha avuto successo?	*Why has Facebook succeeded?*
La raccolta fondi ha avuto molto successo.	*The fund collection has had great success.*

But in normal everyday conversation, **riuscire** would be the best verb to convey the idea of *succeeding*:

È riuscito ad ottenere il lavoro.	*He succeeded in landing the job.*
Sono riusciti a trovare la casa dei loro sogni.	*They succeeded in finding the house of their dreams.*
È riuscita a imparare una nuova lingua.	*She succeeded in learning a new language.*
Siamo riusciti a riavere i soldi indietro.	*We succeeded in getting our money back.*

When used in negative sentences, **non riuscire a** can be used to express *being unable to*, either physically or mentally. Many students say **non posso** (literal translation of *I can't*) when **riuscire** would be a better choice.

Non posso ricordare. ✗	
Non riesco ricordare. ✓	*I can't remember.*

Non riesco a leggere, ho dimenticato gli occhiali.	*I can't read, I forgot my glasses.*
Non riusciamo a spostare il tavolo, vieni a darci una mano.	*We can't move the table, come and give us a hand.*

KNOWING AND BEING ABLE

Speaking of ability and inability to do something, the different uses of the verbs **potere**, **sapere** and **conoscere** deserve a particular mention.

▶ Use **potere** to say what someone can or can't (physically) do:

Elena non può guidare perché si è rotta il braccio.	*Elena can't drive because she has broken her arm.*

▶ Use **sapere** to say that you know how to do something, you have a particular ability or skill:

So nuotare.	*I can swim.*
Sa cucinare Valentina?	*Can Valentina cook?*

▶ Use **sapere** before a phrase beginning with **che** (*that*) or with **se** (if/whether):

So che andate in vacanza domani.	*I know you are going on holiday tomorrow.*
Scusi, sa se c'è una posta qui vicino?	*Excuse me, do you know if there is a post office nearby?*

▶ Use **conoscere** before a noun, or to say that you know or are familiar with/acquainted with somebody or something:

Conosci il poeta Gabriele D'Annunzio?	*Do you know the poet Gabriele D'Annunzio?*
Conosciamo Roma molto bene.	*We know Rome very well.*

▶ But be mindful of the fact that sometimes, particularly in spoken language, **sapere** and **conoscere** are used interchangeably:

Sai la strada per andare alla stazione?	*Do you know the way to go to the station?*
Conosci la strada per andare alla stazione?	*Do you know the way to go to the station?*

39 'In-pressive' mistakes

IMPRESSIVE

Impressive is often translated literally, as **impressionante** or the verb **impressionare**, but in Italian it has a slightly different meaning from that of the English word: it usually indicates something that makes a big impression due to its size, seriousness (as for a serious accident) and generally its negative attributes or consequences.

un incidente impressionante	*a very serious accident*
Il telescopio ha un prezzo impressionante.	*The telescope has an impressive price (a very high price).*
Mi impressiono facilmente alla vista del sangue.	*I get easily upset when I see blood.*
Il film dell'orrore lo ha molto impressionato.	*The horror movie really upset him.*

Here are some examples where it is necessary to find a different way of translating *impress*:

Grazie del regalo. Sono molto impressionato. ✗	
Grazie del regalo. Mi fa molto piacere. ✓	*Thank you for the present. I'm very impressed. (meaning: I'm very pleased/grateful.)*
Le sue parole mi hanno veramente colpito.	*I was very impressed by his words.*

If you would rather use a word that is similar to *impress*, you can do so, but add **bene/buono** or **favorevolmente** to it:

Il candidato ci ha fatto una buona impressione.	*The candidate impressed us.*
Ne sono rimasto favorevolmente impressionato.	*I was impressed by it.*

IN

Learners often translate *in* as the same word, **in**, no matter what its meaning. However, in many cases a different word is needed in Italian, such as **tra** or **a**.

Ho l'esame in un mese. ✗
Ho l'esame tra un mese. ✓   *I've got/I'm taking the exam in one month.*

Vado tra un mese.   *I'll go in a month.*
Finiamo tra una settimana.   *We'll finish in a week's time.*

Another common mistake concerning **in** occurs when it is put in front of the name of a town or a city. Do not use **in** with names of cities, towns or villages; say **a** instead:

Vivo in Londra. ✗
Vivo a Londra. ✓   *I live in London.*

....

Insight

Consider this sentence: *The police arrived in five minutes.*

In Italian, that would be **La polizia è arrivata <u>in</u> cinque minuti,** because in actual fact, **in** stands for 'within' that time period of five minutes.

in = within a time period
tra = at the end of a time period

Ha fatto i compiti in mezz'ora.
It took him/her half an hour to finish his/her homework.

Finisce i compiti tra mezz'ora.
He/She will finish his/her homework at the end of a half-hour period.

....

40 Eventually, earlier and possibly – plus some information and advice

EVENTUALLY

Eventually in English means *in the end* or *at the end*. To express this in Italian, use **alla fine**, **per finire**, or **infine** (more formal).

Alla fine la troveremo.	*Eventually we will find her.*
Dopo aver aspettato tre ore alla stazione, alla fine sono arrivati.	*After waiting three hours at the station, eventually they arrived.*

By contrast, in Italian, **eventualmente** means *in case/in the event of something happening*, or *should ever something happen*. It is similar to **forse** (*perhaps/maybe*), but bear in mind that **eventualmente** expresses a greater degree of uncertainty.

Eventualmente is a good word to use to leave some room for manoeuvre, or to avoid committing oneself to one definite course of action, as it makes things conditional on something else: we're saying we'll do something, but only in the event that something else happens (or indeed doesn't happen).

Sono sicura che andrà tutto bene e non avrò bisogno di te. Eventualmente ti telefono.
I'm sure everything will be OK and I won't need you. If <u>by any chance</u> I do (should something go wrong), I'll ring you.

Eventualmente, se non esci, chiamami.
If, <u>by any chance</u>, you don't go out, call me.

EARLIER

Do not translate *earlier* as **più prima**. In Italian all you need to say is **prima**:

Più prima ho visto Riccardo. ✗	
Prima ho visto Riccardo. ✓	*I saw Riccardo earlier.*

POSSIBLY

Do not translate *possibly* as **possibilmente**, if what you mean is *perhaps*. Translate it instead as **forse**:

– Pensi di finire entro la fine della settimana? – Forse.

– Do you think you will finish by the end of the week? – Possibly.

Possibilmente means something different in Italian: *if possible*. For instance, in a profile on an online dating website you might read:
Cerco una donna giovane, bella, possibilmente toscana.
I'm looking for a young, beautiful woman, if possible from the Tuscan region.

INFORMATION AND ADVICE

Information and *advice* in English are uncountable nouns and don't have a plural. By contrast, in Italian they are mainly plural:

Vorrei delle informazioni.   *I would like some information.*
Mi ha dato dei consigli utili.   *He gave me some useful advice.*

You can also use *information* and *advice* as singular terms but in that case you need a singular article, **il** or **un**:

Devi seguire <u>il</u> consiglio del medico.   *You must follow the doctor's advice.*

Puoi darmi <u>un</u> consiglio?   *Can you give me some advice?*
Volevo <u>un</u>'informazione.   *I wanted a piece of information.*

Scusi, noi volevamo sapere, per andare dove dobbiamo andare, per andare dove dobbiamo andare? Sa, è una semplice informazione.

Se volete andare al manicomio, vi accompagno io!

Totò, Peppino e... la malafemmina, film commedia del 1956

41 How do you 'stay'?

HOW ARE YOU?

It is unfortunate that such a common question as *How are you?* is so often wrongly formulated and wrongly answered, as it is here:

– **Come sei?** ✗
– **Sono bene.** ✗

First of all, *How are you?* should be translated as:

– **Come stai?** *(you – familiar,* **tu** *form)*
– **Come sta?** *(you – formal,* **lei** *form)*
– **Come state?** *(you – plural,* **voi** *form)*

As you can see, **stare**, not **essere**, is the right verb to use here. You can use **essere** with an adjective to describe someone or to say how someone feels:

Mio fratello è intelligente.	*My brother is intelligent.*
È estroverso.	*He is extrovert.*
È contento.	*He is happy.*
È triste.	*He is sad.*

But a question such as *Is your mother OK?*, will translate as:

Sta bene tua madre?

Equally, the answer will require the verb **stare**:

Sì, mia madre sta bene adesso.	*Yes, my mother is fine now.*
No, mia madre sta ancora in ospedale.	*No, my mother is still in hospital.*

Alternatively, *How are you?* can be translated as **Come va?**
(*How is it going?*). In that case, the verb **andare** will also be
used in the reply, or left out altogether:

– Come va?	*How are you?*
– Va bene/Tutto bene/Bene.	*Fine.*

IS IT REALLY?

A related mistake occurs when attempting to translate too literally
the verb *to be* as **essere** in sentences such as:

1 *The jumper is fine. (The jumper fits me.)*
 La maglia è bene. ✗
 La maglia mi sta bene. ✓

2 *Swimming is good for your health.*
 Nuotare/Il nuoto è bene alla salute. ✗
 Nuotare/Il nuoto fa bene alla salute. ✓

3 *It is raining.*
 È piove. ✗
 Sta piovendo./Piove. ✓

Insight

Notice that the expression *it is about to* translates as **sta per**:

Sta per piovere.	*It is about to rain.*
Il treno sta per partire.	*The train is about to leave.*
Emanuela sta per andare a	*Emanuela is about to go and*
vivere a Firenze.	*live in Florence.*

42 Do you visit your friends or examine them?

Consider this sentence:

Ho visitato il medico. ✗

In Italian a sentence like this isn't right as it doesn't convey the right idea: you are in effect saying that you have 'examined' the doctor! How strange, as it is the doctor's job to 'visit' the patient, i.e. ascertain their state of health. This might not be immediately apparent to an English-speaker but it would be so to a native Italian. The verb **visitare** does not mean *to travel from A to B in order to go and see somebody*. It means *to examine*.

The correct version is:
Sono andato dal medico. ✓   *I went to the doctor/doctor's.*

Alternatively, in a more colloquial context:
Sono andato al medico. ✓   *I went to the doctor/doctor's.*

This kind of mistake doesn't hinder communication so it is usually allowed to grow and become ingrained. It then becomes automatic for the English student of Italian to translate the verb *to visit* as **visitare** over and over again, lulled unaware into a false sense of security. After all, the bilingual dictionary will confirm that *to visit* can be translated as **visitare**. But the dictionary can't capture all the nuances of a foreign language, particularly if it's a pocket one.

When making a social call (as opposed to visiting a place or a patient), Italians never use the word **visitare**. They say: **andare a trovare**. This expression is slightly puzzling, given that, translated literally, it means *to go and find*. Surely you don't go and find somebody whom you are just visiting?

From a logical point of view, I can understand why a learner would tend to err on the side of caution and opt for **visitare**. But it would pay off to be a bit more adventurous and aim to get it 100 per cent right: try getting used to **andare a trovare**.

Depending on the occasion, the expression **fare visita** could also be used, but this is a more formal alternative, hardly used in spoken Italian.

It is also possible to use the literal translation of *to go and see* – **andare a vedere**:

Domenica sono andato a vedere gli amici.	*On Sunday I went to see my friends.*

But **andare a trovare** still remains the most common and the truly Italian formula:

Vado a trovare mamma domani.	*I'll go and see my mum tomorrow.*
Vieni a trovarmi presto!	*Come and visit me soon!*

On the other hand, it is right to use **visitare** when visiting a place:

Domani visitiamo la Cappella Sistina.	*Tomorrow we will visit the Sistine Chapel.*

Insight
Il Presidente ha visitato il Papa. *The President visited the Pope.*

Occasionally, it is possible to come across a sentence such as this, in newspaper articles or on TV or in radio broadcasts. But to speak better Italian you should avoid using it yourself.

43 Travel and drive, but don't get too excited ...!

In your excitement about your travels around the country, it's all too easy to use the wrong words to talk about journeys and your reactions. We'll help you get it right.

HOW TO TRAVEL IN ITALIAN

Consider this sentence:

A Natale ho viaggiato a Londra. ✗

The problem with this sentence is that in Italian **viaggiare** has a more limited meaning than *to travel* in English. It is adopted for instance to say what means of transport you use:

Viaggio in treno/in macchina/   *I travel by train/by car/by bus.*
in autobus.

It is also used when somebody covers very long distances, as a professional traveller or explorer would do:

Ha viaggiato per tutto il   *He has travelled throughout the*
continente africano.   *African continent.*

If you just went from New York to Manhattan, London to Paris, or from England to Italy, you haven't covered enough mileage to warrant the use of **viaggiare**! Use **andare** instead:

A Natale sono andato a Londra. ✓   *At Christmas I went to London.*

The verb *to drive*, translated as **guidare**, is another case in point, as it is used far too often, while in Italian its usage is much more limited. In most cases it should be replaced by **andare**. Consider this sentence:

Ho guidato a Londra. ✗

That sentence is wrong because **guidare** tends to be adopted only in specific cases, for instance to say who is going to drive, to comment on somebody's driving skills, to say what happened while driving, how much mileage you've covered or how long it took you:

Domani guidi tu.	*Tomorrow you drive.*
Guida come un pazzo.	*He drives like a madman.*
Ieri mentre guidavo mi sono sentito male.	*Yesterday while I was driving I felt unwell.*
Ho guidato per ore/per 100 chilometri.	*I drove for hours/for 100 kilometres.*

If you want to say *I went by car*, and the fact that you were involved in the <u>act of driving</u> doesn't need to be stressed, use **andare** instead and add *by car*, if necessary.

Sono andato a Londra (in macchina). ✓

FINDING THINGS EXCITING

Exciting shouldn't be translated literally either, given that the Italian word **eccitante** still has the remnants and connotations of 'sexual excitement'. Having said that, it is heard more and more often nowadays in its more generic 'English' meaning. Still, I would advise you to use it sparingly and to prefer in its place the word **emozionante**, or **entusiasmante** which is slightly stronger:

Il viaggio attraverso le montagne è stato molto emozionante.	*The journey through the mountains was very exciting.*
È stata una partita entusiasmante.	*It was a very exciting game.*

44 Please – to be used sparingly, please

Please translates in Italian as:

per favore   **per piacere**   **per cortesia**   **ti/la/vi prego**

La prego is the formal version of **ti prego,** and **vi prego** is the plural version.

In English *please* and *thank you* are ubiquitous; in Italian not as much. This is one of many sociolinguistic differences; it should not make you jump to the conclusion that Italians aren't as polite as people in English-speaking countries. Good manners can be shown in many ways and saying *please* is only one of them, not to mention the fact that, from a phonetic point of view, the English *please* is quicker and sleeker than saying **per favore**!

A case in point: I went shopping in a supermarket in Italy recently, and when it came to the total to pay, the cashier said: **Sono 50 euro e 20.** She didn't say **per favore** or **per cortesia.** She just stated the amount to pay. She wasn't being rude, she just behaved as any member of staff would in the circumstances.

If you order a croissant in a bar, you do not need to say:

Posso avere un cornetto per cortesia? ✗

You can simply say:

Un cornetto. ✓   *(Can I have) a croissant (please)?*

By all means say **grazie** when your order arrives, though again, if you don't say it, people won't consider you bad-mannered or outrageously rude.

On the other hand, if you want to fully affirm your identity as a very kind and well-mannered visitor, do use **per favore** and **grazie** whenever you want! Don't necessarily expect to hear it back from all the Italians you come across – though the chances are some of them will try to reciprocate and be 'overly polite' (as that might appear to them) in return.

Here are two common scenarios in a bar and restaurant:

– Un espresso.	*An espresso coffee, please.*
– Ecco l'espresso.	*Here you are.*
– Mi porta una bottiglia d'acqua minerale naturale?	*Can you bring me a bottle of still mineral water, please?*
– Subito.	*I'll bring it at once.*

To recap, there is no need to pepper your conversation with too many examples of **per favore** or **per cortesia** and **grazie**, unless you want to. You can use **grazie** as much as you want, but do be mindful that you will hear it much less often than in English-speaking countries.

As for **prego**, it can be used in various circumstances: as a reply to **grazie**; when you hand something over to somebody (*here you are*); and to politely encourage somebody to go ahead and do something.

– Grazie.	*– Thank you.*
– Prego.	*– You're welcome/Don't mention it.*
– Posso?	*– May I (come in)?*
– Prego.	*– Please do.*
Prego, si accomodi.	*Please come in.*
Prego, da questa parte.	*This way please.*

The expression **Ti prego** (literally *I pray you*) is used to plead for something:

Mamma, ti prego, mi compri quella bambola?	*Mum, please, will you buy me that doll?*

45 Have you got a title?

In Italian the titles **signore** (*Mr/sir*), **signora** (*Mrs/madam*) and
signorina (*Miss*) are not used as often as their English counterparts.
They are mainly confined to written and formal language, or used
for emphasis.

For instance, if we are angry with someone who has behaved
badly, we might say: **La signora Paola Montereale ne risponderà
davanti al giudice** (*Mrs Paola Montereale will have to answer to
that before the judge*). We call her **signora** with sarcasm: in our
view, she is not a lady at all, or we might be adding the title to
establish as much distance from her as possible.

Two men, Mr Salvi and Mr Nicoletti, greeting each other formally,
would be likely to address each other just by their surname,
omitting **signor**:

– Buongiorno Nicoletti.
– Buongiorno Salvi.

At school, students talking about a teacher whose surname is
Colasanti would refer to him or her as **il Colasanti** in the case of
a male teacher, or **la Colasanti** for a female, or simply **Colasanti**.
They might also call their classmates just by their surname,
particularly those they are not very close to or don't know well.

Gallo è stato bocciato.   *Gallo didn't pass the exam.*

In formal situations, sometimes people address each other by their
professional title and leave out the surname altogether. The most
common titles used in this way are **ingegnere, ragioniere, dottore,
dottoressa, avvocato, ministro, sindaco, commissario, ispettore,
professore, professoressa.**

– Buongiorno ingegnere.   *Good morning, engineer.*
– Salve dottore.   *Hello, doctor.*

In everyday life it is quite common to hear **signore** and **signora** put before someone's <u>first</u> name. Perhaps the speaker wants to sound friendly even though they don't know the person very well or, conversely, they know the person quite well but want to sound respectful. So they would use the title as a mark of respect, while at the same time addressing the person by their first name:

– Signor Antonio, come sta?   *Mr Antonio, how are you?*

If you don't know or don't remember somebody's name, it is of course legitimate to just use a title and say nothing else except **signore**, **signora**, or **signorina**. For instance, to attract the attention of a young lady who has forgotten her bag:

– Signorina, questa borsa è sua?   *Miss, is this your bag?*

Remember that married women generally don't acquire their husband's surname in Italy; they keep their maiden name.

The main defining difference between **signora** and **signorina** is age, rather than marital status. **Signorina** is the right title for a young or young-looking woman, and **signora** is more appropriate for older women, be they married or not. Of course, if you know that a young woman is married, it is appropriate to call her **signora**. And if an older woman is unmarried, **signora** is preferable to **signorina**. As you can see, the titles **signora** and **signorina** are less rigidly defined than their English equivalents.

As for **signore**, when you put it before a surname, do remember to drop the vowel at the end: **Signor Salvi**.

The title **dottore** deserves a special mention, as it is used not only for doctors who have a medical degree or doctorate, but also for anybody with a bachelor's degree, no matter what the subject. As with **signor**, remember to drop the vowel at the end: **il dottor Fazio**.

46 Don't mix c'è with è

There is a strong tendency, particularly at beginners' level, to mix up these two words:

c'è   è

C'è is the combined form of ci + è and means *there is*. È with no subject before means *it is*.

They can also appear in their plural forms, and in past or future tenses of essere:

ci sono *there are*	sono *they are*
c'era *there was*	era *it was*
c'erano *there were*	erano *they were*
ci sarà *there will be*	sarà *it will be*

Here is a typical mistake: a student of mine said <u>they</u> *were too many people*, when what she meant to say was <u>there</u> *were too many people*:

Erano troppe persone. ✗
<u>C'erano</u> troppe persone. ✓   *There were too many people.*

Although there is a clear difference in meaning between è and c'è, the two expressions look and sound so similar that students have some difficulty remembering the difference and therefore tend to mix them up. Here are some more examples of correct use of *there is* and *it is*:

<u>C'è</u> qualcuno che bussa alla porta.	*There is someone knocking at the door.*
<u>È</u> qualcuno che ho conosciuto a scuola.	*It is somebody I knew from school.*
<u>Ci sono</u> due miei amici alla festa.	*There are two friends of mine at the party.*
<u>Sono</u> due miei amici.	*They are two friends of mine.*

Insight

In spoken English, the forms *there were* and *they were* sound extremely similar. In Italian, the difference is more noticeable.

If you are using the <u>imperfect</u> of **essere**, you have **c'erano** for *there were*, and **erano** for *they were*.

Expressing the same meanings with the <u>perfect</u> tense of **essere** gives **<u>ci</u> sono stati/state** (*there were*) and **sono stati/state** (*they were*).

<u>C'erano</u> molte cose da vedere a Venezia.	*There were many things to see in Venice.*
<u>Erano</u> meravigliose.	*They were wonderful.*
L'estate scorsa <u>ci sono stati</u> molti concerti.	*Last summer there were many concerts.*
Ma <u>sono stati</u> cancellati.	*But they were cancelled.*

47 Do you 'prefer' or do you 'favour'?

The verb **preferire** and the adjective **preferito** are often used incorrectly because students tend to assume that saying **preferisco** equates to saying *my favourite*.

Consider this question and answer:

– Qual è il tuo piatto preferito?	*What is your favourite dish?*
– Preferisco le lasagne. ✗	*I prefer lasagne.*

If you reply with **preferisco**, you say something which isn't quite in tune with the question. The reply implies that you have been given a choice of dishes and have decided to go for **le lasagne**. A better answer, more in line with the question, is:

– Il mio piatto preferito sono le lasagne. ✓	*My favourite dish is lasagne.*

If the question in the previous dialogue had been like the one below, then the original answer would have been right:

– Preferisci i cannelloni, gli spaghetti alla carbonara o le lasagne?	*Do you prefer cannelloni, spaghetti alla carbonara or lasagne?*
– Preferisco le lasagne. ✓	*I prefer lasagne.*

Here is another example:

– Cosa preferisci, il gelato alla vaniglia o al cioccolato?	*Which do you prefer, vanilla ice-cream or chocolate ice-cream?*
– Preferisco il gelato alla vaniglia.	*I prefer vanilla.*

Another tip: do not replace **preferito** with **favorito** when you name your favourite dish/colour, etc. Contrary to its English literal translation, **favorito** in Italian has a more limited usage. It is mainly used to indicate:

▶ the favourite in a race, tournament or competition:
Lo davano tutti per favorito   *Everybody thought he was the*
   nella corsa di quest'anno.   *favourite in this year's race.*

▶ the favourite of the sultan in a harem, or the king/queen's favourite:
il favorito della regina   *the queen's favourite*
la favorita dell'harem   *the favourite (woman) of the*
                              harem

The word **favorito** also acts as a past participle (from the infinitive **favorire**), meaning *contributed* or *led to*:

Il grande caldo ha favorito gli   *The great heat contributed to the*
   incendi nei boschi.   *fires in the woods.*

'Preferisco l'italiano!'

48 Time is of the essence

ASKING THE TIME

When asking the time, the question can be either the standard one:

– Che ora è?

... or the slightly more formal one:

– Che ore sono?

Here are two possible answers, one incorrect and one correct:

– Sono le quattro ore. ✗
– Sono le quattro. ✓   *It's four o'clock.*

It is wrong to add **ore** after the number when you say the time.
(You don't need any equivalent of the English *o'clock* or the
French *heures*!)

There is a more formal way of saying the time that does include the
word **ore**, applicable to formal announcements, official timetables
and news bulletins, but then **ore** is placed <u>before</u> the number:

Il concerto si terrà <u>alle ore</u> 11.15.   *The concert will be held at 11.15.*
Chiusura del sottopassaggio <u>dalle</u>   *Underpass closure from 10.00 to*
<u>ore</u> 10.00 <u>alle ore</u> 24.00   *24.00*

> **Insight**
> With the 24-hour clock, do not use the word **mezzo** or **mezza**
> for *half past*:
>
> **Lo spettacolo comincia alle ventuno
> e mezza.** ✗
> **Lo spettacolo comincia alle ventuno**   *The show starts at 21.30.*
> **e trenta.** ✓

LOOKING FORWARD TO

Speaking of time, the expression *I look forward to ...* is often mistranslated as **non vedo l'ora di ...**. The English expression doesn't normally imply awaiting an event with bated breath, but if you use **non vedo l'ora** you are switching to a warmer, more emphatic and emotionally charged formula.

There is no single direct equivalent in Italian, so consider carefully the context and then choose an appropriate turn of phrase, such as one of the choices offered below.

▶ In a formal letter or communication:
   Nell'attesa di un suo cortese riscontro, porgo cordiali saluti.
   I look forward to hearing from you. Best wishes

▶ In a formal conversation, it is sufficient to say:
Arrivederla *or* **Arrivederci**	*Goodbye*
A risentirla	*Speak to you soon*

▶ In an informal exchange:
Ci vediamo presto	*See you soon*
A presto	*See you soon*
A risentirci	*Speak soon*

Of course, if what you really mean is *I can't wait*, then do say:

Non vedo l'ora di rivederti.	*I'm looking forward to seeing you again. (literally, I can't see the hour when I'll see you again)*

Insight

At the end of a conversation or a message, never translate word for word the expression *See you!* or *I'll see you ...* Instead, go for the equivalent of *We'll see each other*:

Ti vedrò il 17 giugno. ✘
Ci vediamo il 17 giugno. ✓   *I'll see you on the 17th of June.*

---

49 Sei single?

In Italian, to say that you are unmarried, you can simply say
sono single, just as you would in English.

Single is one of the many English words that have entered the
Italian vocabulary. By and large most people will use **single** to
say that they are unmarried and without a partner. If you are
looking for an Italian phrase that replaces **single**, you could use the
equivalent of *I'm not married* – **Non sono sposato**, for a man, or
Non sono sposata, for a woman.

You can also say: **Sono scapolo** or **Sono celibe** (for a man), or
Sono nubile (for a woman). Bear in mind that these can sound
rather formal and therefore be more appropriate when you are
filling in a form or giving out your personal details to a civil
servant. The word **scapolo** is also found in fixed expressions
such as:

uno scapolo d'oro	*an eligible bachelor*
uno scapolo impenitente	*an unrepentant bachelor*

Zitella is the non-politically-correct term used to describe an older
unmarried woman, equivalent to *spinster*.

Other useful adjectives for describing someone's marital status are:

sposato/sposata	*married*
coniugato/coniugata	*married (used in more formal contexts)*
separato/separata	*separated*
divorziato/divorziata	*divorced*
vedovo/vedova	*widowed*

A word of warning about using the expression **il mio amico** or **la mia amica** if what you mean is *boyfriend* or *girlfriend*. Using **amico/amica** probably shows the influence of the French words *mon ami* or *mon amie* for boyfriend or girlfriend. What you should say instead is:

il mio ragazzo	*boyfriend*
il mio fidanzato	*boyfriend*
la mia ragazza	*girlfriend*
la mia fidanzata	*girlfriend*

You could also use the equivalent of *partner*, particularly when the individuals concerned are a bit older and the word **ragazzo/ragazza** feels inappropriately youthful:

il compagno	*partner (m)*
la compagna	*partner (f)*

Bear in mind that if you use the word **fidanzato/a**, despite its clear resemblance to *affianced* or *fiancé(e)*, people won't automatically assume you are engaged to get married. This word does imply a greater level of commitment than **ragazzo/a**, so that **fidanzato** could in effect be translated as *steady boyfriend*, but it doesn't necessarily imply that you are going to get married soon.

Insight

In the past, an engaged couple were referred to as **fidanzati in casa**: girlfriend and boyfriend were taken 'home', i.e. introduced to one's parents and relatives, with a view to getting married. Needless to say, this expression and the tradition it originates from have gone out of fashion nowadays.

50a Work, age, and finally ...!

Finally, here are three items likely to come up at some point during conversations in Italy: how to get it right when you say what someone does for a living, when you give someone's age, and when you are recounting events and wish to say *and finally* ....

WORKING FOR A LIVING

Consider this mistake:

Sono l'infermiera.✗

... as opposed to this correct form:

Sono infermiera. ✓   *I'm a nurse.*
or
Faccio l'infermiera.✓   *I work as a nurse.*

When saying what you do for a living, use the definite article (**il/lo/la**) with the verb **fare**; or use the verb **essere** but without the definite article.

If you do use definite articles with **essere**, as in the example above, you are in effect saying: *I am the nurse.* Only if you were to add more information, as in: *I am the best nurse in the hospital!*, would the use of the article be a valid choice, given that, by its very nature, the definite article has a defining role:

Sono la migliore infermiera dell'ospedale! ✓

Now, consider this question and answer:

– *How long have you been working as a doctor?*
– *Since 1990.*
or
– *For 20 years.*

Typically, a student will translate the question wrongly and say:

– **Da quanto tempo hai lavorato come dottore?** ✗

In Italian, using the perfect tense here implies that the person you are asking is no longer working as a doctor. If the person is currently working as a doctor and you want to know how long she or he has been doing the job, you must use the <u>present</u> tense. The sentence below is an improvement over the previous one, but still contains a subtle mistake:

Da quanto tempo lavori come dottore? ✗

It is not quite right because a native speaker would not normally say **lavori come dottore**. They would use the verb **fare** instead – **fare il dottore**:

Da quanto tempo fai il dottore? ✓   *How long have you been (working as) a doctor?*

Notice that the question starts with **da**; this means that the reply will also have to start with **da**:

Dal 1990. ✓   *Since 1990.*
Da venti anni. ✓   *For 20 years.*

Many students will instead wrongly start with **per** (*for*):

Per venti anni. ✗

Here's another example of the difference between **da** and **per**. The first exchange below implies that Arturo still lives in America, while the second implies that he no longer lives there:

– **Da quanto tempo vive in America Arturo? – Vive in America da 10 anni.**   *– How long has Arturo been living in America? – He's been living in America for 10 years.*

– **Per quanto tempo ha vissuto in America Arturo? – Ha vissuto in America per 10 anni.**   *– How long did Arturo live in America? – He lived in America for 10 years.*

Note the use of the present tense in combination with **da** for a state of affairs that is still current, and the use of the perfect tense in combination with **per** for a state of affairs that is no longer current.

50b Work, age, and finally ...!

SAYING HOW OLD YOU ARE

To say how old you are, do not translate literally from English:

Sono 33 anni. ✗

Say instead, 'I have 33 years', i.e. use **avere** (*to have*) instead of **essere** (*to be*):

Ho 33 anni. ✓   *I am 33 years old.*

(If you have learned some French, that experience can help you remember this point, as the structure is very similar: *J'ai 33 ans.*)

You can shorten the answer and just say:

33 anni. ✓
33. ✓

But avoid copying the shortened English form *I'm 33*, because it is wrong to just say:

Ho 33. ✗

'Ho capito

FINALLY

Now consider this sentence:

Siamo stati al cinema, poi al ristorante, e finalmente siamo andati in una discoteca. ✗

If by *finally* you mean *in the end* or *at the end*, do not use the word **finalmente**, say instead: **per finire**, or **alla fine**:

Siamo stati al cinema, al ristorante, e per finire siamo andati in discoteca. ✓
We went to the cinema, to the restaurant, and finally/to finish with, we went to a club.

Finalmente is an emphatic expression and means *at (long) last*. It suggests that you have been waiting for a long time for something to happen.

Finalmente hanno vinto il campionato!	*At last they won the championship!*
Finalmente si sono sposati!	*Finally – they got married!*

Glossary

Adjective An adjective is a word that modifies another word by adding information related to quality, quantity, proximity, distance, or possession:
un maglione <u>rosso</u> *a red jumper*

Adverb An adverb is a word that modifies a verb, an adjective or another adverb. It is invariable: it does not agree in gender and number with the word it modifies:
Paola mangia <u>troppo</u>. *Paola eats <u>too much</u>.*

Article An article is a word that is put before another word (usually a noun) to identify it and specify its gender and number. It can be definite or indefinite. The main equivalent words in English are *the* and *a*.

The definite article is used to indicate a specific, definite person, animal or inanimate object, in order to distinguish it from others. Italian definite articles are *il, l', lo, i, gli, la, le*.
Ho visto <u>il</u> cane di Susanna. *I saw Susanna's dog.*

The indefinite article refers to something in a generic way. Italian indefinite articles are **un, uno, una, un'**.
Ho visto <u>un</u> gatto nero. *I saw a black cat.*

Auxiliary verb Essere and avere are used as auxiliary verbs. Combined with other verbs, they form the perfect tense (**passato prossimo**) and other compound verbs, as well as the passive form.
<u>Ho</u> fatto una torta. *I made a cake.*
Questa casa <u>è stata</u> costruita 100 anni fa. *This house was built 100 years ago.*

Conjugation Verb conjugation consists in declining or changing a verb into its various forms. For instance, to

conjugate **parlare** in the present tense, the ending -are has to be removed. What is then left is **parl**, the stem, to which you need to add the right ending, to get the various forms:
io parlo, tu parli, lui parla,
noi parliamo, voi parlate, loro parlano

- -

Consonant Consonants are letters of the alphabet (excluding vowels) such as B, C, D, Z.

- -

Definite article See Article.

- -

Formal address Adopted with people one doesn't know, or that are more senior or in a role of authority. These people are addressed in Italian using **lei** for *you*. Lei requires third person singular forms, the same as for **lei** and **lui** (*she* and *he*).

Nowadays it is rare to express this formality in the plural; therefore if you are talking to more than one person in a formal setting, all you are likely to need is the **voi** form. Occasionally the very polite **loro** form might be used by staff in exclusive restaurants and hotels.

- -

Gerund A gerund is commonly known in English as an -ing verb. In English it ends in -*ing*, in Italian it ends in **-ando** or **-endo**. It is used with the verb **stare** to refer to an action in progress, happening at the time of speaking or changing and developing at the present time.
Il mio italiano sta <u>migliorando</u>. *My Italian is improving.*
Sto <u>scrivendo</u> il glossario. *I am writing the glossary.*

It can also indicate temporary actions or situations:
Sto <u>lavorando</u> nell'ufficio di mio marito fino a quando non ritorna dalle ferie la segretaria. *I'm working in my husband's office until the secretary comes back from her holiday.*

- -

Homograph When two words look the same but have different meaning and function.

<u>Ve</u>stiti, è tardi! *Get dressed, it's late!*
Ho comprato due ve<u>sti</u>ti estivi. *I bought two summer dresses.*

. . . .

Imperative The imperative is a verb form used to give orders, instructions, make suggestions and give advice:
<u>Va</u>da sempre dritto. *Go straight on.*

. . . .

Indefinite article See Article.

. . . .

Indicative The indicative is a verb mode or mood that indicates certainty. It is the normal form used, contrasting with the conditional and the subjunctive.
George parla inglese. *George speaks English.*

. . . .

Infinitive The infinitive is the basic form of the verb as given when you look a word up in an English–Italian dictionary:
parlare (*to speak*).

In Italian, infinitives are divided into three main groups depending on whether they end in **-are**, **-ere** or **-ire**, for instance: **parlare, ridere, partire** (*to speak, to laugh, to leave*).

A very small group of irregular verbs ends in **-rre**, such as **produrre** (*to produce*).

. . . .

Informal address Informal address is adopted with people you know, family relations, friends, young people and children.
The singular form is **tu** – the second person singular.
The plural form is **voi** – the second person plural.

. . . .

Intransitive verbs See Transitive and intransitive verbs.

. . . .

Noun A noun is a word used to name a person, an animal, a place, an inanimate object, an abstract idea or an action:
un elefante *an elephant*   **l'email** *email*   **un'idea** *an idea*

. . . .

Object An object usually comes after the verb and shows who or what is affected by the verb. It can be direct or indirect.

In the sentence **Sandro ha dato <u>un regalo</u> a <u>sua moglie</u>** (*Sandro gave a present to his wife*), **un regalo** (*a present*) is the direct object and **sua moglie** (*his wife*) is the indirect object.

Either or both of the objects can be replaced by a pronoun before the verb, so that the sentence becomes **Sandro <u>le</u> ha dato un regalo** (*Sandro gave her a present*) or **Sandro <u>l'</u>ha dato a sua moglie** (*Sandro gave it to his wife*).

If both pronouns are used, they combine to form **glielo**: **Sandro <u>glielo</u> ha dato** (*Sandro gave it to her*).

. . . .

Partitive article This indicates an indefinite part of a whole and is formed by merging the preposition **di** with the appropriate definite article. These words often translate as *any* or *some* in English:
Vorrei <u>dell'</u>acqua. I'd like <u>some</u> water.

di + il = del	di + lo = dello	di + la = della
di + i = dei	di + gli = degli	di + le = delle

. . . .

Past participle A past participle is a verb form used in compound verbs, especially in the perfect tense.
Ho <u>fatto</u> una scelta. *I made/have made a choice.*

. . . .

Personal subject pronoun A pronoun is a word that replaces a noun. A personal subject pronoun replaces a proper or common noun that is acting as the subject of the verb in the sentence. In English, the subject pronouns are *I, you, he, she, we, you, they*. In Italian they are **io, tu, lui, lei, noi, voi, loro**. (See Chapter 17.)

. . . .

Possessive pronoun A possessive pronoun replaces a possessive adjective and noun. In the sentence **È il mio libro** (*It's my book*) **mio** is a possessive adjective, whereas in the sentence **È mio** (*It's mine*) **mio** is a possessive pronoun.

Plural A plural is a form of any word that expresses a quantity greater than one: **le ragazze** *the girls.*

Preposition A preposition is a word like *of* or *in* that links a noun, pronoun or infinitive to other elements of a sentence. It has a specific function which varies according to the context and the meaning of the words it serves and its place in the sentence.

A preposition can be simple (i.e. monosyllabic and invariable): **a** (*at*) **di** (*of*) **da** (*from*) **in** (*in*) **su** (*on*) **con** (*with*) **per** (*for*) **tra/fra** (*between*)

A simple preposition can combine with a definite article, as shown in the table below.

	il	lo	l'	la	i	gli	le
a	al	allo	all'	alla	ai	agli	alle
di	del	dello	dell'	della	dei	degli	delle
da	dal	dallo	dall'	dalla	dai	dagli	dalle
in	nel	nello	nell'	nella	nei	negli	nelle
su	sul	sullo	sull'	sulla	sui	sugli	sulle

Reciprocal verb Reciprocal verbs are identical to reflexive verbs in their form but they express a reciprocal rather than a reflexive action: the action is exchanged or done mutually, to 'each other' or to 'one another'.
Dario e Livia si sposano domani. *Dario and Livia are getting married tomorrow.*

Reflexive pronoun Reflexive pronouns are an integral part of reflexive verbs such as **lavarsi** *to get washed.*
<u>mi</u> lavo   <u>ti</u> lavi   <u>si</u> lava
<u>ci</u> laviamo   <u>vi</u> lavate   <u>si</u> lavano

Reflexive verb In reflexive verbs the subject and object of the sentence are the same: **mi lavo** (*I wash myself*). They require a reflexive pronoun, which is an integral part of the verb form. (See Chapter 33.)

Relative pronouns A relative pronoun links or 'relates' two phrases together. (See Chapter 20.)
Conosci la ragazza <u>che</u> porta il vestito blu? *Do you know the girl who is wearing the blue dress?*

Subject A subject often comes before the verb and is the person or thing that performs the action, is in a certain state or feels a certain feeling expressed by the verb. The subject dictates the actual form of the verb. In the sentence **Sandro telefona a sua moglie** (*Sandro phones his wife*), **Sandro** is the subject of the verb.

Superlative A superlative indicates a quality or characteristic at its highest level. In English, *fastest* and *smallest* are superlatives.

Transitive and intransitive verbs A <u>transitive</u> verb has a direct object. With a transitive verb you can get an answer to the question *who* or *what*. An example is **mangiare: Mangio una mela.** (*<u>What</u>* do I eat? I eat an apple.)

An <u>intransitive</u> verb doesn't have a direct object and doesn't allow the question *who* or *what*. An example of an intransitive verb is **andare: Vado a casa.** *I'm going home.*

Verb A verb is a word used to describe an action, state, feeling or relation, such as **cantare** (*to sing*), **essere** (*to be*), **sentire** (*to feel*) or **avere** (*to have*). Those examples are in the infinitive form; to use them, they have to be changed to the correct person and tense, to communicate information about 'who' and 'when'.

Vowel Vowels are letters of the alphabet (excluding consonants): A, E, I, O, U.

Index

Numbers refer to chapters 1–50 of this book.